POLITICAL CORRUPTION AND POLITICAL GEOGRAPHY

This book is dedicated to the victims of political corruption.

Political Corruption and Political Geography

PETER JOHN PERRY
Reader in Geography,
University of Canterbury, Christchurch, New Zealand

Ashgate

Aldershot • Brookfield USA • Hong Kong • Singapore • Sydney

Published by
Ashgate Publishing Limited
Gower House
Croft Road
Aldershot
Hants GU11 3HR
England

Ashgate Publishing Company
Old Post Road
Brookfield
Vermont 05036
USA

British Library Cataloguing in Publication Data
Perry, Peter John
   Political corruption and political geography
   1.Political corruption 2.Political geography
   I.Title
   364.1'323

Library of Congress Cataloging-in-Publication Data
Perry, Peter John.
   Political corruption and political geography / Peter John Perry.
      p.   cm.
   Includes bibliographical references and index.
   ISBN 1-85521-901-8
   1. Political corruption. 2. Political geography. I. Title.
JF1081.P47   1997
364.1'323--dc21   97-1226
                                           CIP

ISBN 1 85521 901 8

Printed and bound by Athenaeum Press, Ltd.,
Gateshead, Tyne & Wear.

Contents

List of Figures (Cartoons)

Preface

This is an unhappy book, even though I have enjoyed writing it. It is unhappy by reason of its subject matter, a matter so generally depressing - political corruption has done almost nothing to increase the sum of human happiness - that generations of scholars, geographers among them, have generally ignored it. The aim is then to expose the scandal of wilful scholarly concealment - sometimes called the 'too hard basket' - of what is one of the driving forces of the world's political systems and political geographies at every scale from global to parochial. The scandal is more evident in political geography than in any other domain and it is to that audience that the book is particularly but not solely addressed, seeking to convince that corruption matters, that as a political process it is at least as important to geography as its counterparts such as due legal process. Since the scandal is *inter alia* a matter of ignorance as well as of convenience the book cannot take the form of a closely argued account of the connexions between political corruption and geography. Before such an account can be essayed, firstly a general discussion of the phenomenon of political corruption must be provided, not least because popular opinion widely and diversely misunderstands and misrepresents it, to which only secondly can be attached an initial and introductory account of interrelationships. Nor on the other hand is a comprehensive account of political corruption required, such as Heidenheimer, Johnston and Levine supplied in 1989, a true handbook as its sub-title claims. Rather I seek to introduce the subject in terms appropriate to my field and my colleagues and to begin the task of generating discussion: first words rather than last. My interest in the subject began in the early 1980s with a dissatisfaction born of experience in undergraduate teaching. A lengthy gestation has taken the project into a period when throughout the world the phenomenon of political corruption has become more and more conspicuous, its political significance widely recognised, and public opinion generally, albeit often confusedly, hostile. (There is almost the danger that by comparison with the early periods of this change in status political corruption will be taken for granted.) What remains is for the scholarly community at large, and geography in particular, to wake up and catch up: the role of this book is to sound the essential reveille.

Christchurch, New Zealand
November 1996

Acknowledgments

This book could not exist without the help I have had from numerous colleagues, a wide circle of friends and a supportive family. Some of the most important cannot even be named for fear of the consequences to them and their families: for this reason some material in the text remains unreferenced. Their direct and indirect help is gratefully acknowledged from the comfort and security of an office desk in what is, at least by reputation, an almost corruption free country. Colleagues in the Department of Geography at the University of Canterbury have always been willing helpers, listeners and critics in a friendly and stimulating environment. The technical and secretarial staff of the department have been invariably helpful, especially Linda Harrison who has typed numerous drafts and revisions. The University of Canterbury generously granted study leave in 1993 when most of the reading was done. In more general terms it remains an institution where curiosity driven scholarship, unencumbered by the demand for proposals and approvals, has an evident place: long may this essential of the university remain. Scholarship depends on libraries and I have welcomed the predictable, but I hope never taken for granted, expertise and helpfulness of librarians in general and especially at Canterbury and Cambridge. Permission to reproduce cartoons from *The Economist*, *Times of India*, Burkhard Mohr (*Frankfurter Allgemeine Zeitung*) and *The Guardian* is gratefully acknowledged. Transparency International came into existence more or less as I began this book and the materials which it publishes have been a precious resource, so too the interest of Jeremy Pope its Managing Director who read and helpfully commented upon an early version; as also did Andrew Church of Birkbeck College, London University while an academic visitor to Canterbury. My subject matter is not an easy one from the publisher's perspective and so I thank Dartmouth and its staff for their support. Together we have made this book: responsibility for what it says remains with the author alone.

List of Abbreviations

FEER   Far Eastern Economic Review

FT   Financial Times

NYT   New York Times

SEAM   South East Asia Monitor

SMH   Sydney Morning Herald

1 Political corruption: introduced and discussed

Most of the scholarly disciplines which might *a priori* be expected to have a great deal to say about political corruption - political science, economics, sociology for example - in fact say very little. There remains an 'unwritten section on graft' to quote the cogent observation of *The Economist* in 1957 (*Economist*, 15 June 1957). The paraphernalia of academic success and respectability, books, articles, journals, conferences, research grants, are few and the sole specialist journal - *Corruption and Reform* - lasted less than a decade before in 1993 it was absorbed into another - *Crime, Law and Social Change*. Resort to abstracting journals or the indexes of books on places and subjects where corruption has an evident role produces similarly frustrating results. (Perhaps the very structure of many disciplines marginalises the topic?) Such results are a better indicator of the topic's scholarly status than are the bibliographies constructed by the authors of books on the subject, impressive and wide ranging as they may be. For whatever reason - several are proposed below - there is a huge disparity between the real world significance of political corruption and the amount of scholarly attention which it receives.

Experience provides a different perspective. In many parts of the world everyday corruption on a modest scale does not even have to be sought out. The evidence is there on the streets to say nothing of only slightly less public manifestations, in the Post Office and the police station for example. Petty corruption, small scale payments to officials for services which ought to cost nothing, is in many countries commonplace and endemic. Grand corruption, of cabinet ministers and senior officials, may often be less immediately conspicuous (though this is commonly not the case with the proceeds) and it is also part of the experience of a smaller segment of the population but it too is widespread and of more fundamental significance. As I began reading for this book early in 1993 Italy and Japan in particular featured in these latter terms on an almost daily basis in Britain's quality press. Five years earlier Italy merited six such entries in the index to the *Financial Times*. Corruption of a similar kind in the third world has lost much of its newsworthiness by repetition. As I revise this text political corruption appears to exist on an even wider scale.

Events since 1993 have almost completely cut the ground away from both popular and scholarly complacency. It ought no longer to be possible in Britain for example for serious newspapers to argue the unimportance of political corruption even if it remains the case that Britain is probably less corrupt than Italy let alone say Nigeria. Recent spectacular examples are common enough, Westminster, Lambeth for example; but recall also that two decades ago, between 1974 and 1980, corruption trials explored and exposed the governance of five British cities and thirty smaller authorities, scarcely evidence that corruption is a new issue formerly of little significance (Gillard and Tomkinson, 1980, viii). New Zealand has had a similarly complacent tradition exploded by the ongoing Cook Islands tax evasion scandals and by rumours as to the integrity of the planning process in the Auckland region. In both Britain and New Zealand, and probably more widely, a growing belief in the corruptibility of the political system is one foundation among several of a high level of popular political cynicism. There are very good reasons to believe that political corruption is a stronger and more widespread force than politicians and civil servants would by word or action have us believe. After all they have a vested interest in minimising the problem just as journalists and the media are open to the reverse accusation. All this is to argue a vital role for the scholar and to lament his or her as yet insignificant contribution.

Most scholarly authors claim to write about neglected situations or at least to cast new light upon those as yet but partly explored. The first of these claims certainly applies in this case and is a reason for writing this book; it is compounded by a second - practical importance. This book has no claim to be a manual of practice or prevention; but nor can it deny the subject matter's real world significance. Knowledge of how corrupt politics and administration works is in many countries a matter of life or death. How to work the system, how to get round it, how to expose it to public view and how to combat it all operate on such terms. The subject has a practical dimension. A third matter is equally important and less obvious - the extreme intellectual challenge of the topic. As the book unfolds the reasons why corrupt politics and related geographies are much harder to study than the honest versions will become evident. That intellectual challenge is the best of reasons for any work of scholarship, but after three decades at work on topics of limited immediate usefulness I gain some satisfaction in even a rather theoretical approach - I think I have been bribed only once in my life but of course I can never be sure - to a serious and understudied real-world issue. For it is no longer uncommon to find political corruption in a significant place in studies of for example third world poverty, where its role was often suspected but rarely articulated thirty years ago; the same is true of communist régimes in Europe and their collapse. In other words the depressing situation outlined at the very start of this book is beginning to change for the better, at least inasmuch as corruption is taken more seriously, even while and in part because its incidence probably goes on increasing. This book aspires to a place in that beginning, from and for the geographer's perspective - of which more anon - but first there is a great deal more to learn from the period and circumstances of wilful neglect.

Scholarly neglect is not something new in this context. There never has been a strong tradition of scholarly enquiry into political corruption save perhaps in parts of Europe (Huberts, 1995, 316-7) and the world of public affairs has generally been portrayed in unrealistically honest terms. The absence of such scholarship is surprising. Noonan (1984) for example, writing on the more specific but very closely related theme of bribery, notes its absence from United States legal writing between 1900 and 1970 (1984, 536-7) and, by contrast, from post-Reformation theology (1984, 538-43), geographical and historical contexts where bribery was evidently of significance. Bribery, Noonan also notes (1984, xvi) is one of only two crimes mentioned by name in the United States constitution. (The other is treason (Reisman, 1979, 3).) Rose-Ackermann observes in Heidenheimer's vast overview of the subject that 'the simple expedients of corrupting the inspector or juggling the books are seldom part of the analysis' (Heidenheimer, 1989, 661). The International Political Science Association Index has no entry under corruption for the period 1950-75, a cogent indicator of its lowly intellectual standing. What such absences indicate is not only disinterest, public and maybe influential complacency, but also methodologies which self-perpetuatingly ignore or marginalise the topic. The situation continues: Hawkesworth and Kogan's *Encyclopaedia of Government and Politics* (1992) lacks a main entry for corruption and is content with five very superficial references. By contrast Alatas (1993) provides a short but cogent piece for the *Oxford Companion to the Politics of the World*. Almost unbelievably a 1994 text (Furlong, 1994) on Italian politics has two index entries on corruption. However one leading authority on Italian politics of recent decades, La Polambara, might reasonably be described as a convert from scepticism and complacency (La Polambara, 1964, 295-6) to a rational belief in the seriousness and significance of the phenomenon (Transparency International, 1994, 75-89). He is simply the best known among several such. Positivist and to a degree Marxist approaches, albeit for different reasons, are especially prone to subdue and eliminate discussion of corruption. The evidence is rarely such as to allow rigorous testing of hypotheses, and the phenomenon of corruption appears to be not only largely independent of modes of production but ubiquitous. In brief, disciplines which should have a lot to say about corruption generally and for various reasons say very little. This is not an explanation: it is to expand upon a deficiency in scholarship which calls for an explanation. The topic is dirty, difficult, dreary and disagreeable for sure, but that is not the explanation. If it were then war and domestic violence might be expected to be understudied. In fact the reverse is the case. What then is the explanation?

When that question is asked it must first of all be admitted that enquiry into corruption, journalistic or scholarly, raises extraordinary practical and methodological problems largely outside the experience of geographers in other branches of the subject and of scholars in general. There is an obvious risk of violence as a way of stopping the researcher from finding out, or in retaliation. An interview with a locally well known writer on issues of this kind in an English town was conducted in a 'fortified' garden shed because he had good reason to fear for the safety of himself and his evidence. He was careful, possibly eccentric, but certainly not irrational. In other countries more extreme precautions are needed. More generally the whole question of data collection is problematic. Orthodox field work is the exception; subterfuge and concealment are as necessary for researcher as for practitioner. (I am not sure what response universities, other funding agencies and their ethics committees might give to this aspect of any request for support.) The result is scholarship often dependent on the work of others, on journalists in particular skilled and courageous in the discovery and presentation of deliberately concealed data. This is not to argue that scholars cannot and should not investigate but rather it is to note the inapplicability of much standard social science methodology practice and data, the pre-tested questionnaire and the carefully constructed sample to say nothing of official statistics for instance. The heartland of the evidence is commonly the domain of rumour and anecdote. And in Coke's words (Cecil, 1964, 107-8), over three hundred years ago, when Lord Chancellor Bacon was tried for corruption: 'in such works it is a marvel that there are any witnesses'. The evidence is a tiny part of the totality.

More fundamentally all our data, anecdotal or otherwise, is unrepresentative, and unrepresentative to an unknown and unknowable degree. The perfect cases of political corruption - and such probably exist - are those of which even the existence is unsuspected. Apparently 'clean' communities may in fact be very 'dirty'. A recent example of the generally unsuspected coming to light is the $2 million corruption case against a cantonal restaurant and bar inspector in Zurich (*Neue Zürcher Zeitung*, 6 April 1994 to 18 September 1996). The honesty of Swiss officials has generally been taken for granted. There is then no place for elegant numerical models (if very occasionally some room for abstraction) and even our verbal models will be tentative and approximate. Occasional citations of a number, a percentage rake off, the size of a bribe must be treated with caution. Such stories may lose little in the telling but on the other hand strong forces are at work with a vested interest in downplaying the scale of corruption. Above all the relation of particular to general is unclear. Holmes (1993, 146) observes: 'all that is being analysed here is *reported* corruption; this may or may not correlate closely with actual corruption. If it does not - and there is no way of knowing this - then it is even more questionable to make correlations'. This is unfamiliar ground to the geographer, but not quite so unfamiliar to the archaeologist, the ancient historian (and even the historical geographer) seeking to explore an inaccessible world on the basis of non-random fragments.

If these difficulties look like good grounds for abandoning enquiry before it is begun, especially to scholars of a post-modernist or positivist persuasion, there is more and worse to come. At the heart of corruption are such issues as deceit, lying, secrecy and subterfuge, themes rarely, on their own admission, explored by philosophers let alone by a diversity of disciplines, from anthropology to sociology, in which their role is central. Historians go so far as to recognise the importance of these issues as part of the human condition without according them any centrality, but at least they are in their recognition of the importance of corruption far ahead of geographers. Only one discipline appears to focus strongly on such issues - accountancy. Bok (1978, 5) writes that a 'reluctance to come to grips with deception can stem from an exalted and all-absorbing preoccupation with truth'. (And I would add order.) Interestingly and alone among substantive writers on corruption Waquet (1991, 104-18) devotes a whole chapter to lies. However as Markovits and Silverstein (1989, 258) point out: 'it is the fact of concealment that enables us to distinguish genuinely scandalous behaviour in politics from the merely incompetent, simply stupid or stubbornly wrong headed'. The intractable methodological issues have a positive dimension which we must later address.

A third methodological problem, the least often discussed, is the very status of corruption. It has traditionally nearly always been seen, and usually condemned, as aberrant behaviour and abnormal process, as anomaly or residual, as secondary or non-vital. In contemporary Eurocentric terms and despite a recent apparent increase in the incidence of corruption in many western democracies - which may or may not correspond to a real increase - this remains a defensible position, capable also of support in terms of the logic of proceeding from the healthy to the morbid. On a global and historical view it is harder to justify. For most of the world's population and for most countries corruption plays a significant, and not infrequently the most significant, part in the process of political decision-taking at all levels. A Martian intellectual commissioned *ab initio* to give an account of earth politics - and perhaps too a thoroughly committed empiricist - might just as well start here as with the rule of law and its honest administration.

Scholarly neglect of political corruption then owes much to practical and methodological difficulties. It is not only the most blinkered survivors of the quantitative revolution who are persuaded that these are insurmountable and that the topic is thus inappropriate for scholarly enquiry. But for some of us the real world importance of the issues and the intellectual challenge disqualify the arguments rehearsed above. Geographers are committed to study the world as it is not the limited part of the world which currently fashionable methodologies believe it is possible or appropriate to handle. After all journalists and a few scholars have met with success in their studies of corruption, not merely by satisfying peers and reviewers in the latter case but in the former attaining the high standards of proof required in the courts and even occasionally contributing to topple (and reconstruct) corrupt administrations. They have provided raw materials, foundations and examples of scholarly enquiry into corruption, demonstrating that the problems may be real but are surely not overwhelming.

What has been said above remains an incomplete account of the intellectual neglect and marginalisation of the topic. It is not only difficulty but also complacency which has this effect both upon scholars and also upon governments and administrations, complacency compounded by ignorance and malice, and even by political correctness. Thus Alexander and Caiden (1985, 149) comment upon: 'textbooks on US public policy and administration where one looked in vain for any account of public immorality, official lawlessness, bureaucratic deceit, administrative corruption, and the subversion of government by special interests'. A decade later this is no longer quite so much the case. There is also the complacency of affluence and influence, of cosmetic cures wherein successful action against a conspicuous few engenders relapse into inertia. It is not however a coincidence that corruption has risen up the public agenda of awareness at a time of economic recession and collapsing social and political confidence in western democracies (and not only there), where complacency was most evident and the role of corruption most often denied. Very occasionally a country publicly and realistically recognises the seriousness of the problem and acts accordingly. Corruption was officially deemed one of the three great evils in China in 1952, alongside waste and, significantly, bureaucracy, and ahead of bribery (a sub-set of corruption), tax evasion and theft of government property (Fitch and Oppenheimer, 1966, 118). The agenda was more political than philosophical, hence the conceptual overlaps, but evidence suggests that for a time it was acted upon to good effect, a remarkable achievement in the Chinese context. Ironically corruption is now resurgent even rampant in China.

Complacency is not however a total explanation for the neglect by scholars of corruption, especially in the second and third worlds. In the communist case there was some initial success in reducing corruption and the official line that such campaigns had succeeded and that it was impossible for corruption and Marxism to coexist proved remarkably durable. For most of the period of communist rule external access to reliable information was controlled, and scholars who wrote about the communist world were either sympathisers inclined to discount rather than believe evidence of corruption, or of a hostile persuasion and focused upon seemingly more important targets. The local press and legal profession were subject to constraint. Corruption in these countries and eventually and evidently on the grand scale was for these reasons only slowly and belatedly exposed to the rest of the world. The local populations were well aware of what was happening at a much earlier date since corruption was for them both a burden and a survival mechanism - to introduce a very important distinction - in a failing social and economic order, and thus a growingly important dimension of everyday life. As an increasingly public scandal at the highest political levels corruption contributed to the dramatic turn of events of the later 1980s.

In the third world the extent of corruption was - it scarcely remains - an equally well kept secret. Here corruption in the loosest sense is indigenous, much older than European contact or colonisation. All empires appear to suffer from low level corruption and not a few, the later Roman Empire and Belgium in Africa for example, were totally permeated. As far as the British Empire is concerned many authorities note an evident growth and expansion of corruption at all levels during World War Two in a context where scarcity and shortage were coupled with fast growing political aspirations - a situation not unlike the last decade or so of communist Europe - and that this corruption flourished as and after independence was gained (Fitch and Oppenheimer, 1966, 48-52; Monteiro, 1966, 30-8). What was evident to residents and visitors was however ignored by all but a few scholars. Myrdal, a Nobel prize winner in economics and certainly not unsympathetic to newly independent states was among few prepared to point up the paradox:

> Although corruption is very much an issue in the public debate in all South Asian countries ... it is almost taboo as a research topic ... the explanation lies in the general bias that we have characterised as diplomacy in research ... the taboo on research on corruption is indeed one of the most flagrant examples of this general bias (Myrdal, 1968, 938-9).

Change has been far from complete. *The Economist* reports on 5 March 1994:

> In public the (World) Bank tiptoes delicately around state crookery, scarcely mentioning the word 'corruption', and never in the same breath as an individual country.

To be fair a new chairman may bring in radical change in this context (*FT*, 2 July 1996). The Commonwealth only began to discuss the topic in 1990 and it does not feature in the 1995 Millbrook Declaration. It is also worth noting that the *Far Eastern Economic Review*, a benevolent apologist in the 1960s (Engels, 1993, 14) now strongly asserts the opposite position. To return to Myrdal (939), he went on to comment on prevailing explanations of third world corruption: universality, colonial heritage, economic necessity and utility. Chapter 20 of Myrdal's *Asian Drama* remains a classic account of third world corruption. But a form of political correctness still serves to some degree to marginalise corruption, and one particular interpretation of the history of the last century or so added to the present world economic order is seen completely to satisfy the need to explain present day third world dilemmas, corruption included. Explanations of particular economic and social problems in such terms as bribery and nepotism still run the risk of accusations of patronising neo-colonialism or even racism even when they admit the role of the colonial past, and attempts are still made to exclude them from the intellectual and practical agenda, ironically in countries which are not themselves among the most corrupt. The exceptions are few and courageous, most notably in addition to Myrdal they include two French agronomists, again of the political left, Dumont and Mazoyer

(1969), of roughly the same period as Myrdal, and whose work now appears equally prescient and visionary. Nor was it ever quite impossible to find indigenous refutations of the explanation of corruption in terms of colonialism (Monteiro, 1966, 68-9). Now a growing number of local political and intellectual leaders see corruption not only merely (and conveniently) as a legacy but rather as a long standing problem as much entrenched in the present as inherited from past social and political and economic orders, and in need of present remedy if sustainable growth is to be achieved (Ayittey, 1992).

Let us summarise. Corruption has been ignored by scholars and statesmen because it is conceptually problematic and because to recognise its real importance is inevitably to challenge both the *status quo*, intellectual as well as political, and some of its powerful beneficiaries. External and historic causes have shouldered too large a part of the burden of blame and explanation, largely because politically correct attitudes have been so powerful in this area especially *vis à vis* the third world. The end of that unfortunate and disgraceful situation has begun, and this book hopes to be part of the end of that beginning.

One other problem requires preliminary discussion and anticipates the question of definition shortly to be discussed. It may however precede it, for however clear the definition it is never easy to disentangle political corruption from other irregular political processes, chance (good or bad), incompetence and indolence for example. These last two are widely and accurately regarded as breeding grounds for corruption but are not to be equated with it. Rose-Ackermann (1978, 4) lists no fewer than seven processes standing between government policy and its implementation, an incomplete list in my view but two members of which (nepotism and corruption) fall within my definition of corruption. This book's thesis is that by comparison with rule following (or legal process) as the reputedly healthy political norm - and the central or even sole concern of most political geographers - corruption and the other 'irregulars' are too important to be neglected. Corruption's pre-eminence among the 'irregulars' arises from its uniquely rich element of intention. Corruption does not just happen: it sets out to achieve a different, distinctive, particular and for its perpetrators rewarding outcome; it has villains and victims.

A brief digression, a comparison with elections and electoral geography, here suggests itself, not least as the absence of corruption from the established agenda of political geography contrasts so sharply with the highly inflated, in my view, status of elections. As occasional, public, and even exciting events which may generate political change and certainly generate a mass of statistical data, elections attract scholarly attention as well as media hype. There is moreover money in electoral research. Elections are conspicuous, even central, within recent political geography even though in much of the world they exist in no meaningful form. Their results in the medium and long term are often modest in terms of social and economic change compared to the level of scholarly attention which they receive. By contrast political corruption is covert, continuous, almost ubiquitous and often inconspicuous. The result is minimal funding, low if growing public awareness and modest scholarly activity. But this author has no doubt as to which is the more practically significant and intellectually demanding field of scholarship.

To return to the mainstream of discussion: an emphasis on corruption neglected has its risks. The extreme form is a kind of reductionism: we pursue bribery and graft through the literature and in the field and end up with a body of material whose status is exaggerated by its extraction and separation from a broader political context. Instances of complete takeovers by corruption are rare, present day Zaire, some North American cities a century ago: the scholar's task is generally to understand corruption as an important part of a larger whole. To do this he or she must understand not only corruption but its context of honest and legitimate politics and administration. Even when not thus reductionist there are related risks, the invocation, on a flimsy evidential basis, of corruption as a way of completing an incomplete explanation, of eliminating 'noise' or 'residual', of convenient explanation for the inexplicable (Summers, 1987, 12). In placing too large an explanatory burden on corruption it is too easy to forget the presence and pressure of chaos in the real political world and its essential irreducibility. There is finally the likelihood, especially in ideological terms, of finding what we look for (Williams, 1987, 100-1): the Marxist sees in corruption a means of capital accumulation, the liberal a reaction to regulation. In neither case does an ideologically blinkered analysis reach the core issues.

When that has been said it is equally appropriate to end this introduction by reasserting the inadequacy of many intendedly holistic analyses, geographies among them. Look for example at almost all geographies of France and the United States, and the nothing they have to say on corruption. (Moreover they are often so structured or argued that it would be difficult to say anything. Indexes provide a simple demonstration of this point although a cautionary note as to undue dependence is in order: not all compilers of indexes are competent or imaginative.) Popular recognition of the reality of corruption as a potent social force demands its interpretation to and by geographers and its incorporation in their work.

2 Defining political corruption

To this point the possibility and need for definition has been assumed, but none has been provided. To do so is not easy. At the one extreme a handful of scholars take up the task and seek for a definition which couples precision and circumscription while avoiding an undue restriction on their licence to explore a territory of rich diversity. At the other extreme such vacuous phrases as 'all politics are corrupt' are the commonplaces of everyday conversation. They will crop up whenever and wherever the scholar whose interests are in corruption goes public and interacts with a non-specialist audience. They tell us nothing more than that politicians and civil servants are often unpopular and in many instances are also regarded as untrustworthy and materially (to say nothing of intellectually) dishonest. Nor are observations such as Lethbridge's (1985, 5) that especially in America corruption represents 'the "institutionalised" influence of wealth in a political system' operationally helpful, cogency and perceptiveness notwithstanding.

Scholarly shortcomings are of a rather different kind. Firstly there is simple omission to include corruption in definitions where it obviously belongs, a particularisation of the general argument rehearsed in chapter one. Thus the Task Force on Organised Crime of the (US) National Advisory Committee on Criminal Justice Standards and Goals falls short in its definition of organised crime (an important sub-sector of corruption) by failing to incorporate the generally essential role of corrupt officialdom (Alexander and Caiden, 1985, 9). A second commonplace shortcoming is in essence no more than careless usage where meaning varies on a page by page basis. Two otherwise excellent books exemplify a conjunction of penetrating insight and loose and variable definition: R. Sandbrook *The politics of Africa's economic stagnation* (1985) (despite a useful definition) and J. MacGaffey *Entrepreneurs and parasites: the struggle for indigenous capitalism in Zaire* (1987). Typically, in these instances and elsewhere, the word is linked with others which are either a sub-set or an overlapping phenomenon: 'fiscal largesse and corruption', 'nepotism and corruption'. Maintaining consistency of definition in practice is extremely hard to achieve and the flaw in these two books is far from fundamental, but the need to define remains essential and its exploration is intellectually stimulating. Flawed definitions also occur in legislation: that in Britain's *Prevention of Corruption Act* (1906) was tautological, and its 1916 successor assumed (on the basis of receipt of a gift) what it ought to have defined (Chibnall and Saunders, 1977, 145-6).

An etymological approach

The multiplicity of the meanings of the words 'political' and 'corruption' is however as much a part of the English language as a licence for muddled thinking, and the two words 'political' and 'corruption' do provide an etymological starting point on the road to definition. Firstly there is in the word corruption an element of breaking, rupture or separation, applied in the political context to legal or customary norms. The fact that corruption can become a dominant process does not invalidate this insight for it is very difficult to find cases where bribe or backhander would be viewed as the official or acceptable legal standard. The prefix 'co' in the original Latin is an emphatic, asserting thoroughness and completeness. In present day usage the word also has a transactional connotation - the 'deal' between at least two sometimes many more parties. Thirdly the word signifies, again from a Latin root, rottenness, decay, degeneration; from this comes the 'rotten apple' or 'bad egg' analogy often used when the phenomenon is being explained in terms of individual behaviour. Hence also is derived the frequent albeit not unanimously accepted analogy of corruption as a pathological condition, a 'decision pathology' in Reisman's (1979, 6) telling phrase - locational decisions among others - and as such of invasive and infectious tendency. It should be noted however that none of these are intrinsically unnatural processes. Collectively they focus our attention upon illegal or irregular transactions (the breaking of rules or trust, bad deeds) to the detriment of the public good and by which one party unfairly gains at the expense of the other. This last only tenuously derives from etymology but is certainly central to the idea of political corruption where material, usually monetary, transfer, and thus loss and gain, are an essential objective and feature. However a distinct yet parallel dimension focuses the scholar's attention, like that of the operator, upon not money but power. The association is most famously, albeit inversely, expressed by Acton (1956, 335): 'power tends to corrupt'. Watergate is the most famous, but not necessarily typical, recent instance. This facet of political corruption when compared to the material aspect raises even bigger definitional problems. Corruption for material and monetary gain has reasonably exact and evident frontiers by comparison with that which seeks empowerment. When and where do political dirty tricks lose the last vestiges of legitimacy or legality? When power is incorporated into the definition there is a risk that the topic will become unmanageably large and imprecise and the argument developed in the first chapter that corruption is a neglected topic will start to collapse. Yet the quest for power undoubtedly overlaps with its material and monetary counterpart. Some authorities strongly assert the separation, Markovits and Silverstein (1988) for example; this book emphasises the monetary and material element without totally excluding the other.

Political is a simpler but equally important word. It serves to separate out corruption as essentially related to government from crime in general. It is not what you do but where and who you are that defines you as politically corrupt. Most acts of political corruption at least bend and more often breach the rules and a large proportion are crimes, but there are good reasons, as diverse as the broad implications on the one hand and the pivotal roles of deception and secrecy on the other, for the consideration of political corruption separately from crime, and these reasons are of general and not merely geographical application. 'Political' of course focuses our attention on state and government, legislature, executive and judiciary interacting with one another and the community, keeping the rules or breaking them on both sides. Some of its connotations are obvious - public works, prime ministers - and others less immediately so - postal officials, land-use planning for instance.

The role of experience

Etymology takes us some way: experiences the rest. They are so integral to the topic that some have already been mentioned: deception, subterfuge, lying, cheating - unfamiliar ground for most scholars. As Woodrow Wilson (Bok, 1984, 8) observed: 'secrecy means impropriety'. As has already been noted really successful corruption is totally unsuspected corruption, a situation which pushes us to the edge of any definition. The question of secrecy possesses however one especially important implication - all that can be studied is flawed examples. Further, as Schleifer and Vishny (1993) point out, it is the essential role of secrecy in corruption which confounds an interesting argument that well organised corruption does less harm than a disorganised, 'everyman (or woman) for him/herself' situation. The presence of inequality also calls for comment both as a necessary element ('I have what you need - material goods, a service, and not least information - and don't have: and it's for sale'). Thus corruption, at every scale above the personal or individual, perpetuates and accentuates rather than diminishes social, economic and thus spatial inequality. That last word is its objective: 'what corrupt business wants from government is not efficiency but privilege' (Alatas, 1990, 169). Lastly the bald idea of corruption as theft must be stated. Someone or more often several parties get what the rules do not entitle them to. 'Someone' is quite the appropriate word: the widespread and determinedly anonymous role of personal contacts often receives comment (Benson, 1978, 34). There is however a danger of over emphasis on individuals and understatement of the even more elusive patterns and systems, of an emphasis on rotten apples rather than bad barrels or diseased trees. Nevertheless corruption is more realistically viewed as a network of deals among individuals than as a system of entries in ledgers or even notebooks. After all much of it proceeds by word of mouth and hand to hand.

When all these issues have been discussed the last hurdle of an actual definition remains. Lowenstein (in Heidenheimer, 1989, 30-1) finds five elements in United States federal and (most) state law which help us to proceed: public officials, corrupt intent, benefit, official act, influence. This is a useful checklist for both instances and definitions. Gardiner and Lyman (1978, 5), again in a United States, but mainly municipal, context suggest 'exchange of money or other material goods for preferential treatment by public officials'. Alatas, a Singaporean working in a broader context, proposes simply 'abuse of trust in the interest of private gain' (Alatas, 1990, 1) a little more cryptic and arguably needing the adjective political before trust. These are sufficient formal definitions for our purpose, but Alatas' (1990, 1) list of nine essential elements is also worth citing at this stage: trust betrayal, deception, subordination of common to specific interests, secrecy, involvement of several parties, mutual benefits (material or pecuniary), a focus on decisions and decision makers, concealment or camouflage, and a contradictory dual function undertaken by both the giver and receiver of the bribe or its equivalent. This last requires explanation: for an act to be corrupt, Alatas argues, it must involve a contradiction between what is legitimate and what is not within the same operation, issuing an import licence for example.

Some questions

Definition circumscribes the subject but with a fence of uneven height
and doubtful impenetrability. It leaves us with definitional questions as
well as answers. The most immediate, not necessarily the most
important, of these is of the distinction between legitimate lobbying, a
necessary and ubiquitous political activity, and illegitimate influence,
bribery and corruption. Summers links the two when he describes
bribery as the lobbyist's last resort (1987, 93). Chibnall and Saunders
(1977, 139) quote John Poulson, a central figure in one of Britain's
most publicised corruption scandals: 'just what is entertaining and what
is corruption?' The United States Congress has recently (1994)
examined this topic. Most people can in this context distinguish
between a business lunch and a Caribbean cruise but would have
difficulty in placing an exact line across the middle ground. It would
also seem intrinsically more difficult to do so at the top, at say senior
executive level, than for the dustman or the doorkeeper. There are
similar problems in countries in which the tradition of gift giving is
widespread and long established. However, several friends from the
third world have scathingly commented upon the element of self
deception among practitioners of corruption when we have discussed
limits and definitions, a view echoed by Lethbridge writing on Hong
Kong - 'people do not drift into it unwittingly' (1985, 22-3). The line
is hard but not impossible to draw to know and to enforce. When it
comes to public discussion in contexts where both law and custom
make definition difficult public opinion may nevertheless clearly
differentiate in terms of acceptability, a situation supporting my
friends' position. In Japan for example the emphasis lies upon clear
violation of the law, personal enrichment via dishonesty, bureaucratic
corruption, and unseemly behaviour by national leaders as detrimental
to legitimate government (MacDougall, 1988, 224-7).

Nor does a restrictive definition rule out discussion of fine, even
seemingly unhelpful, distinctions. The European Union's Common
Agricultural Policy is infamous for a high level of fraud, at least
hundreds of millions and probably several billion dollars a year. On
our definition only that uncertain but undoubtedly substantial part
where a government official has deliberately participated for profit,
rather than having been deceived or merely incompetent, falls within
our ambit. Surely this class of fraud needs looking at as a whole
without doubtful benefit of fine distinctions? But exactly the same can
be said about political corruption at large which without distinctions
and definitions becomes a shapeless and unmanageable topic. There is
room for both lines of enquiry and geographers should need no

persuading as to the merits of exploring issues from a variety of perspectives and will continue to echo Sauer's ringing denunciation of a concern for proprietary, exclusive and limited intellectual rights: 'this way lies the death of learning' (Sauer, 1941, 4). Definitions are to be put to work, not merely to have their finer points debated. The question of definition is however of operational as well as intellectual significance. At the time of final revision of this text (October 1996) *The Times* (14 October 1996) reports the situation that a very prevalent form of political corruption - in essence 'speed money' - is viewed by Britain's Audit Commission (the main investigating body) as maladministration rather than corruption. This ruling has been challenged but the effect is to rule out criminal proceedings and to restrict redress (via the Ombudsman) to compensation.

Most significant and most difficult is the matter of context, of time and place. Is what is political corruption here and now also political corruption there and then? Does acceptance of a plurality of cultures and discourses, central to geography in its general tradition and presently particularly alive in the form of post-modernism in particular, either invalidate the concept of corruption or restrict what we have to say to formal description? The folly of evaluating say eighteenth century British elections, notoriously corrupt to our eyes as well as to that generation, in twentieth century terms is self evident. It does not however mean there is nothing worthwhile to be said about them in the context of a general discussion of corruption even though law and popular opinion have changed. (This is however one reason why historical examples appear rather infrequently in this book and only when they have a special pertinence to a present day or conceptual issue.) Is it similarly foolish to look at contemporary Kenya, distinctly corrupt, in terms of the norms and practices of say Norway (almost certainly reasonably 'clean'). In this case there is some difference in law but a much greater difference in private and public attitudes between the two. Again an affirmative answer to the question, of cultural relativism, is quite defensible and in one sense intellectually essential. We can only understand Kenyan corruption to the extent that we can begin to understand, ideally enter into, the hearts and minds of its practitioners, accepting that Kenyans and Kenya differ from Norwegians and Norway. But that process only too readily opens out into a cultural explanation of corruption and into justification as well as explanation of politically corrupt activities which are by any standards, including those of indigenous faiths and cultures and not merely those of the West, unjust, unfair and oppressive. It may also become an excuse for both outside business involvement and political non-intervention, but as Elwert (1993, 17) observes 'foreign partners cannot excuse their contribution ... by citing a "normality" in African societies', a normality I would add which if it exists is a recent accretion of spurious legitimacy in terms of longer standing traditions. Obasanjo (*FT*, 14 October 1994) and Ayittey (1990, 44-5) comment in the African context that the phenomenon of corruption is in fact perversion of an age-old tradition of moderate, regulated and open gift giving. The cultural defence of corruption is then if anything even more offensive to Africans and Asians than an assertion of the superiority of liberal Western values. Alatas (1990, 95), Singaporean and Muslim with decades of third world experience, accuses the relativists of misunderstanding and distorting the cultures which they try defensively to invoke. 'It is true that traditional societies stress the kinship bond, but I have never come across any traditional value system that encouraged immoral conduct as a means to help kin.'

Definition is not then without its difficulties, both intellectual and operational. The need to provide, and to try to remain within, a workable definition does not pretend there are no problems. (Almost for certain I have fallen short in this respect.) Nor is it a claim to exclusive rights. Rather it asserts that for corruption to be the object of our study, a legitimate object for intellectual enquiry, its definition must be explored and debated, and that while the eventual definition is important this is equally true of the wide ranging discussion which precedes it.

3 What political corruption has to do with geography

Geography is a discipline which claims, as its name suggests, to be rooted and grounded in the real world. The area of political corruption is one area where that claim does not stand up well to scrutiny. The very little which geographers have said - they have a modest presence in my bibliography - is then a very insecure starting point. If we narrow the domain of discussion to political geography then as that sub-discipline focuses upon power and political process so political corruption requires what it has in fact never received, a central place in its philosophies and procedures. But that requirement must not safely and cautiously peripheralise political corruption: it belongs in the mainstream of geography, in its theoretical and its applied branches, and in historical as well as contemporary geography.

In geographical as well as in general terms however this book is not (as has already been argued) an exercise in reductionism: it does not seek to explain political corruption substantially in terms of geography or *vice versa*. Rather it seeks to establish a place and role for political corruption in the now several mainstream geographical traditions and to emphasise the importance of overviews, interactions, syntheses and connexions, in such a way as to enhance understanding both of geography and of corruption.

The title of the book is deliberate: the time for a more exact and extended treatise on the political geography of corruption, a study of corruption within a political geography framework and/or of the place of corruption within geographical scholarship is not (quite) yet. This book takes a looser position, exploring the connexions between political corruption and place while also hoping to expose geographers to a range of ideas about corruption. This appears necessary both on account of the modest extent of present geographical scholarship - and I suspect the limited empirical knowledge of most geographers - concerning political corruption and because to understand the connexions geographers need a general as well as a particular understanding of political corruption. A further reason for such an approach is that popular discussion of corruption is so often methodologically vacuous or naïve in such diverse aspects as right or wrong, functional or disfunctional and even as to its extent.

In the area of political corruption more than in most branches of geography we need to know in rather exact terms where we have come from, even where we might have been - in Myrdal's phrase 'to establish the ingredients' (Myrdal, 1968, 942) - before we can speak with authority about where we are at and where we are going. At a risk of misleading readers this book might well have been called *Corruption for Geographers: an exploratory manual*!

A concern for place

A persistent and fundamental feature of geographical scholarship is a concern for place, for what constitutes place, for what makes place characteristics and place differences (Johnston, 1991). Quite evidently political corruption is a place characteristic and a spatial variable. It is in this as in every respect notoriously difficult to quantify and equally notoriously the domain of rumour and anecdote. At one extreme it is so salient a feature of particular places that a rational geographical discussion of certain places which claims to be in any sense comprehensive must incorporate or even be driven by a consideration of corruption or be deemed seriously defective. Contemporary Nigeria (*Economist*, 8 June 1996) or the great cities of later nineteenth century North America provide examples. The same may be said of particular categories of places, ports and border crossings, micro-states with an involvement in laundering the proceeds of various illegal activities and - more controversially - major administrative centres. At the other extreme all the evidence suggests its insignificance in contemporary Singapore and New Zealand, although as has been noted there are evidential peculiarities in the context of corruption which counsel caution as to such judgements. Systematic exemplification is arguably harder in this case than in the reverse situation: perhaps university cities are an apposite example?! In between there are countries parts of which are deservedly regarded as more corrupt than others, a geography calling for explanation: Georgia in the old USSR (Clarke, 1983, 261), a phenomenon based on both culture and environment; the north-east Henan and the Hong Kong border in China (Holmes, 1993, 145). In all these circumstances, and at the centre as well as at the extremes, the corrupt condition of a particular place may be viewed as a dependent variable explicable, albeit never totally, in terms of a range of other and independent variables even if their interpretation will always be controversial. But corruption may also be viewed as an independent variable; it is one of the features of everywhere (arguably even in its near absence - this is often commented upon as one of the remarkable features of Singapore) which contributes to the character of particular places and must figure in any analysis. For example the relatively greater economic growth in southern by comparison with northern China in recent years has been attributed to a lower level of corruption which in turn rests upon the existence in the region of fewer state protected enterprises with a vested interest in corruption (Cheung, 1996, 3-4). Corruption may then be viewed as both cause and consequence. Such questions as why were and are some North American cities and states evidently and notoriously more corrupt than others, and how do variations in the extent and form of corruption contribute to the different place character of say the several Australian states and metropoles or the various West African countries are equally legitimate. Not all scholars carefully however construe the dependence-independence difference and its misunderstanding has sometimes been claimed to invalidate analysis (Charlton, 1990, 23).

A concern for difference

A complementary focus arises from the simple fact that place differences provide differences of both need and opportunity for corruption. Thus Gardiner and Lyman (1978, 10) writing of planning corruption in the USA note the place specific component as a result of differences in rules, contexts and attitudes from place to place. As Williams writing on Africa in 1987 (77) observes: 'local conditions shape the form and extent of corruption'. And he goes on to provide a salutary caution against sweeping generalisations since similar local conditions do not always generate similar local outcomes. Thus the contemporary third world provides different opportunities from the communist or ex-communist world, Benin from Bulgaria for example, but also and less easily and obviously explicable Guinea from Ghana, New Jersey from New York.

A second persistent feature of geographical scholarship is then a concern for difference: geography makes a difference - geography explores difference: geography is context and geography is consequence. Without corruption many geographies at many scales would not be what they are - the railway network of Victoria (Cannon, 1966, 39-46), law enforcement in Lima (de Soto, 1989), land-use around the Birmingham conurbation. This is essentially a counterfactual - a comparison with what might have been in different but not totally different circumstances - a form of argument implicit in much of geography but infrequently articulated in detail by comparison with say economic history. Ironically it is within geography and in the corruption context that despite its methodological significance it is usually an argument available only in principle. Maps of tramways and housing, disease and 'vice' as they would have been had the game been played by the rules are theoretically possible and intellectually fascinating but, on account of the shortcomings of the evidence, they are practical impossibilities in most cases.

The differences are of course of reputation as well as of reality. In a world where establishing the realities of corruption is notoriously difficult the reputation of places as well as of people is what matters, and reputation is often far removed from actuality. Again we are on familiar geographical terrain, summed up in the word perception. The investor in south-east Asia, for the first time especially, encounters not hard facts on corruption but a mixture of fact, rumour and speculation, and it is these which are the basis for his decisions: likewise the tourist in his or her quest for the 'thrills and spills' of the 'red light district' or, even more dangerously, in his or her relationship to the forces of law and order in a strange land, two areas where a corrupt element is commonplace.

Geography in general

This is to begin an account of how political corruption relates to the several schools of thought within modern geography. In some instances the issues are substantially practical: the characteristic data for the study of corruption is rarely such as to enable construction of rigorously testable numerical models even though hypothesis testing in a broader sense may be quite practicable. Certainly in the domain of rumour and anecdote the role of rigour as an antidote deserves emphasis. The Marxist account, at least in its more traditional version, is in some respects less of a problem: class is self evidently a significant element in corruption (to be discussed later) and corruption may legitimately be viewed as class driven, class creating and class sustaining. Its role becomes more problematic firstly when the uncertain but not insignificant role of corruption in the downfall of Europe's communist régimes is considered. These were of course Marxist only in a loose sense and a Marxist fundamentalist might well argue that corruption is well viewed as among their fatal flaws. The most serious weakness of this kind of Marxist analysis (but not of some recent variants (Clark and Dear, 1983)) is in its emphasis on the pre-eminence of the material over the ideal or the moral. Corruption is a materially driven phenomenon, a manifestation *inter alia* of human greed for money and goods, but also for the less tangible power and prestige. However, there is to acts of corruption a moral and ideal as well as a material dimension, moments of individual decision but not necessarily of identical decisions in even very similar circumstances and for which moment and moral issues the Marxist account may leave too little space. The implication of this argument is then that there is room also for humanistic and idealist accounts of corruption within geography and more generally; some will pursue this path only in terms of collective ideas and material situations, others in more individual terms, but in each case seeking to get as far as possible inside the minds and motives of the participants.

The domain of post-modernism and its acceptance of the plurality of cultures and discourses raises other problems in the corruption context. Some post-modernist writing appears curiously arrogant on this point: 'there is no longer *terra incognita* in our political geography' (Heller and Fehér, 1988, 6). But the same authors, despite a post-modernist distaste for general theory, are still able to put forward lists of civic virtues which they deem universal and which including as they do civic courage, justice, and rational discourse leave ample scope for consideration of corruption (88). The same is true of their emphasis (122) on the consistent and continuous application of rules as essential to the idea of justice. Scholars who see themselves as heirs of the Enlightenment may have less difficulty - but may perhaps too naively assume an uncritically condemnatory role - in accepting the concept of corruption within their scholarly paradigm. Ironically the whole process of the Enlightenment is surely one of the major causes of corruption's diminishing role in the west during two centuries, and the very recent resurgence of political corruption in the liberal democracies perhaps serves as an indicator of that intellectual position's malaise. To summarise, it is not impossible to find a defensible and workable place for corruption within those schools of thought which comprise contemporary geography. In some it is so obvious as to call for no comment, empiricism (woolly or otherwise) and pragmatism for example. Elsewhere its place is one which while it contributes to our ideas may yet be subject to practical and/or methodological constraints and generative of tensions and contradictions.

Political geography in particular

Is the same to be said of political geography? As with geography at large so too here the evidence is non-existent rather than equivocal. The essential reason for this book is that political geographers have had so little to say about what even a cursory examination reveals as a potent force. If we take as a starting point the various attempts to produce procedures and structures which combine eclecticism and order, Pounds' text (1963), Cohen and Rosenthal's article (1971) for example, and most recently Glassner's text (1993) where at last corruption almost begins to be substantially treated, then there is no obvious problem. The same is evidently true for attempts, notably by Slowe (1990), to organise political geography around the theme of power. Even had there been no Lord Acton the compatibility would be self-evident. More generally any methodology with a place for process can readily accommodate corruption even if it does not initially do so. This is not the case with usually older methodologies emphasising morphology. The relationship of corruption to the view of political geography first propounded by Taylor in 1985 (Taylor, 1993) and now for just over a decade widely influential within the field is less apparent. The emphasis on the global scale pushed onward into the revival of geopolitics is unpromising territory for subject matter with so strong a local personal and interpersonal component. However it must also be recognised that political corruption functions at a global as well as at local, regional and national scales. Global institutions, the World Bank for example, examine the extent to which they might cooperate with corrupt governments. Multinationals may provide essential support - even if only by failing to actively condemn as with Shell in Nigeria - for corrupt régimes in important countries, or in the case of banks may provide the essential services for political corruption. It has evidently been equally in the interest of greater powers at least to prop up corrupt client régimes, in francophone Africa for example. As the new political geography focuses upon the new world order so then the role of corruption needs to be asserted in such contexts as third world development, multinational business and the international arms trade. The overall problem remains: it is not that attempts have been made to integrate political corruption into political geography and failed - they have not yet been tried.

The other major thrust of contemporary political geography is that focused upon theories of the state. Again corruption does not feature in the index of such a classic as Clark and Dear *State apparatus: structures and language of legitimacy* (1983) but it is none too difficult to insert corruption into its analysis, to see for example corruption as a highly individual and alternative way of participation in the capitalist state or as an expression of dissatisfaction with the forum role of the capitalist state as an arbiter of disputes and conflicts. Clark and Dear have no difficulty in deciding how the state legitimately differs from such rivals as the Mafia (188), an especially cogent example in the context of this book. The state is not legitimised solely by its democratic institutions but by an altruistic concern for more than itself, by practices and institutions 'designed to advance the good of its members' - a concern intrinsic to the study of corruption - 'and effectively regulated by a public conception of justice' (188) which is so evidently absent from political corruption. Our moral evaluations of corruption are in fact often driven by context: if the theory and practice of a particular state be benevolent or altruistic corruption will be condemned as immoral. But evidently many states cannot accurately be so described and our evaluation of corruption in these situations is necessarily driven by estimation of the extent and role - sometimes total - of the deficiencies of particular states and their élites in this respect and by comparison with alternatives both real and hypothetical. This is not to defend the role of corruption as a practical solution in such cases even when in practice it may turn out to be less bad than the official situation and legitimate alternative while yet inferior to other possibilities. But it is to permit at least estimates of its role as not intrinsically and inevitably the worst possible case and to provide a basis for a broader understanding of its role - its geographical role included - than one which is uncritically condemnatory.

4 Political corruption: characterised and described

Corruption introduced, corruption defined, and corruption related to the discipline of geography set us on the path to characterisation and description. The latter destination is obvious if all too often dismissed as elementary. But what of characterisation? What is meant here is the emphasising of particular and significant features, otherwise too easily overlooked, by such means as analogy, antithesis and epigram. Not every field of scholarship merits such an approach but one of the few appealing features of this intrinsically dismal topic is the wealth and richness of such material, a wealth of insight, a wealth of substantive comment, a wealth of methods for its investigation, even a wealth of wit.

The most famous of all characterisations is one of the briefest: 'power tends to corrupt and absolute power corrupts absolutely' (Acton, 1956, 335). The dictum is often misquoted, in which process the tentativeness of the first part is lost, and it always occasions surprise that it first appears in a letter.[1] It is now more often cited as warning than as analysis: we assume its validity and endorse it as good advice for would be reformers. Its numerous critics, notably Rogow and Lasswell (1963), and contradictory manipulators remain relatively unpublicised: 'powerlessness corrupts' (Hook, 1980, 41); 'corruption kills power' (Sarassoro, 1980, 215-6); 'corruption indicates where power is' (Williams, 1987, 52); 'corruption as exchange of wealth for power' (McMullan, 1961, 504). In all of these there is a whiff of reductionism, of the over simplification of a covert and complex process. By comparison the not quite so famous observation by Gibbon (Gibbon, 1776-8, chapter 21) - 'the most infallible symptom of constitutional liberty' - is monumentally obscure, at least to this generation. What he is asserting is however of some importance: a vote, an office, or a decision for sale - as certainly was commonplace in eighteenth century Britain, exaggeration notwithstanding - represents 'constitutional liberty' as opposed to an unstructured and arbitrary authoritarian alternative.[2]

Analogy

By comparison present day scholars favour analogy and the most popular of these is pathology (or in more general terms disease). To cite but one example Taras (1986, 150), writing of Poland in the Solidarity era, views corruption in Poland as a pathological condition comparable to alcoholism or drug abuse. The usefulness of the analogy rests both in itself and in the objections and qualifications which it has aroused. Firstly note the at least questionable assumption of a norm of honesty and of corruption as an abnormal departure. Our Martian visitor might see things differently! As to the infective, invasive and potentially life threatening character of corruption, to resume the analogy, there is more consensus. Objectors to this kind of analogy have often worked in third world situations where corruption is commoner than honesty and shows no signs of being a passing or terminal condition. It should also be noted however that the situation where most of a population is afflicted with a particular ailment does not vitiate the very concept of pathology. The extreme of criticism is simply to stand the procedures of this book and the pathological analogy on their heads and to set out to enquire into and account for the exceptional condition of political honesty, and to regard corruption as a normal 'way of constituting the state' (Mèdard, 1990, 74). One more sophisticated version of the pathological analogy - parasitism - carries useful connotations of corruption as load or burden and in its more technical and sophisticated forms, commensuality - sharing a common table - for example, figuratively enhances our understanding.

Other terms are used similarly although discussion is less fully developed: McMullen (1961, 184) equates corruption and divergence; Simis (1982, 177) views corruption as alienation, appropriately so vis-à-vis the USSR. Markovits' and Silverstein's (1988, 264) preference for pollution over pathology in this context instinctively appeals to geographers not only on grounds of familiarity but also in its connotation of disturbance of a preferred, but not necessarily natural, order (the political and administrative eco-system), of the wide ranging and unforeseen results of particular acts, and of the diversity of control measures extending well beyond simple pesticides. Rosenthal (Heidenheimer et al., 1989, 702) in the more commercial and international context observes that corruption erodes the ideal of competition (hence the keenness of United States' concern). This analogy significantly links the seemingly superficial with the deeply menacing. Myrdal observes 'corruption puts sand in the economic machinery' (1968, 932), and the idea of corruption as friction appears

in the later writings of Steffens (cited by Noonan, 1984, 584), one of
the best known investigators of municipal corruption in the United
States. The simplest of all one word analogies comes from McGaffey
(1987, 211), a sceptic as to pathology and a defender of the
functionality of corruption in admittedly extreme circumstances -
glue. Glue has its place, in the furniture for example, but emphatically
not in the engine room, to assert by comparison the lubricant analogy.

For me the richest, most striking (and most entertaining) of all
analogies appears in a now generally forgotten book written by C.H.
Garrigues: *You're paying for it: a guide to graft* (1936, 2-3).
'Whenever a government activity moves through a charged field and
into "lines of influence" created by private business, graft is generated,
just as electricity is generated whenever an electrical conductor cuts
into lines of force of a magnetic field. And induced corruption, like
the induced electricity, can be used to turn the wheels of progress - to
the material advantage of the owner of the wheels.' Garrigues was an
inevitabilist rather than an apologist: the book is extremely practical,
almost 'tongue in cheek' and instructional. Interestingly the dynamo
analogy sees corruption as a form of energy more useful than
dangerous. He does not extend it to include electric shock. It is
surprising that this analogy has not been picked up and worked upon
by other scholars: McKitrick's (1975, 511) passing and undeveloped
mention seems to be the sole exception.

Epigram

Analogy then has a place in sharpening our understanding of
corruption and so does the often epigrammatic attempt to convey its
essence in a single sentence or phrase. Some appear initially trite but
less so on reflexion: the idea of corruption as a parallel or
complementary system; Doig's (1984, 380) remark that corruption is
not an end in itself; corruption viewed as an alternative to violence
(Scott, 1972, 35), as distortion, as the elimination of competition
(Clarke, 1983, xvi). Others are of a more evident profundity. Leff
(1964, 11) interprets corruption as a 'hedge against bad policy', de
Soto (1989, 154-5) as an 'insurance against uncertainty'. Here
elimination or at least reduction of risk features as a motive. Lippman
uses the phrase 'traffic in privileges' (Heidenheimer, 1989, 568).
Gould (1980, 122) views corruption as privatisation of the state -
hence warnings that this is one of the risks inherent in privatisation as
government policy - and Waquet (1991, 73) as the disintegration of
the state. Although in many respects a functionalist apologist for

corruption he also observes that 'moralisation, lies and casuistry ... are the three columns on which the reality of corruption was built' (1991, 142). Note the suggestion of self-deception. Shapley (1889, 54), an American satirist writing in the heyday of municipal corruption suggested three different words - 'addition, division, silence'. Finally there is the memorably ambiguous phrase 'honest graft' usually employed, as it originated, in a North American context to describe and justify a way of getting things done which need doing and which otherwise would not get done. Noonan (547) claims that the concept begins with George Washington. It is an embryonic and particular version of the functionalist account and defence of political corruption. It is a particularisation, central to the functionalist defence, of the view of corruption as a lubricant. Typically 'honest graft' is concerned with modest corruption at the municipal level in such areas as public works, often in the form of advance information. 'Sure there's some graft, but there's just enough to make the wheels turn without squeaking. And remember this. There never was a machine rigged up by men didn't represent some loss of energy ... the theory of historical costs you might put it. All change costs something. You have to write off the costs against the gain. Maybe in our state the change could only come in the terms in which it was taking place, and it was sure due for some change' (Warren, 1946, 417).

FAZ, 24 July 1995

Anthithesis

Lastly there are a number of thought-provoking antitheses. Scott
(Heidenheimer, 1989, 135) and many others distinguish between
corruption in making the rules and in putting them into practice
between political corruption and administrative corruption.
Transparency International differentiates between 'corruption
according to rule' (having to pay for what you are entitled to - the
general category of which 'speed money', discussed elsewhere, is a
commonplace example) - and 'corruption against the rule' (paying for
what you should not). The distinction between grand and petty
corruption is commonplace, between corruption of the minister, a
matter of hundreds of thousands of dollars, and corruption of the
minor official, for as little as a few dollars. The two, rich/poor and
grand/petty are not identical, but as Wade (Ward, 1989, 75) points out
connexions between the two are revealing. High level corruption
generally renders low level corruption inevitable: the tone is set at the
top. But the reverse is not true: Britain's colonial empire experienced
almost ubiquitous low level corruption but very little at the highest
levels. In the French post-colonial context Mèdard (1986, 118-9)
distinguishes between parochial (traditional, often nepotistic or
familial) corruption and market corruption - the bribe as a mere
business transaction. Development he argues engenders a move from
the former to the latter. Then what? Also in a third world context Ekeh
(Ekeh, 1975) distinguishes between two publics, the 'private public'
advantaged by corruption, and the larger 'public public'
simultaneously disadvantaged by the same process. His phrase the
'kinship corporation' also deserves mention (Davidson, 1992, 226).
Scott (1972, 143) contrasts the short term redistributive role with its
long-term function as an inhibitor of growth or change. Holmes
(1993, 65) writing on the USSR distinguishes 'grass eaters' - passive
recipients - from 'meat eaters' - active solicitors. Gardiner and Lyman
(1978, 116-25) distinguish between the opportunistic and the more
serious organised versions. Eisenstadt sees its basis in a struggle
between individuality and community (1978, 218). Prasser (1990, 65)
argues, on lines intrinsically appealing to geographers, for a focus on
networks rather than events. Gardiner and Lyman (1978, 202)
comment that 'corruption involves more than a few dollars changing
hands between sleazy individuals'. Van Klaveren (Smith, 1964, 195)
stresses the systemic element. They and many others are in fact
discussing elements or perceptions of more general antitheses which
can be severally and summarily expressed: a conservative or

subversive force; lubricant or friction; functional or dysfunctional; a debate taken up in a later chapter.

To state and survey, to begin to explore analogy, anthesis and epigram is to anticipate as well as to illuminate substantive discussion. The concluding chapter will *inter alia* return to assess their usefulness and validity. They are presented here not as a mere parade or *tour de force* but because the conceptual and imaginative richness of the topic, so often viewed in dismal and pragmatic terms, is one of its important and unexpected features. As Shahid Alam (1989, 443) points out however, in cautionary mode, this kind of discussion of political corruption tends to run ahead of in depth case or systematic study, but at least it may qualify a fragmentary particular and anecdotal approach and force us to connect particular and general. Characterisation then usefully precedes description, the essential task of the rest of this chapter, but illuminates rather than supersedes it.

Description

Geographers have traditionally, at least in recent times, regarded description as an elementary even a menial task, Sir Clifford Darby's (Darby, 1962) memorable assault on this point of view notwithstanding. They have either taken it for granted or ignored it. In the case of political corruption a large number of people of whom scholars are a miniscule minority would lay claim to some knowledge and understanding, but what is it that they know and how can it be stated? For certain no one has a comprehensive knowledge from Abu Dhabi to Zimbabwe, and invaluable as such an encyclopaedia or yearbook might be, as universal description it does not equate with geography. Geographical description prefers systematisation and synthesis to comprehensiveness and especially favours the case study. The issue and the need are the more acute when the subject matter is one where neglect, misunderstanding, misrepresentation and mythology abound, as in the case of political corruption. Our starting point here is a broad brush geographical overview and synthesis followed by several case studies connecting our preliminary rather general discussion (much of which is not specific to geography) to a more analytical and systematic treatment more geographical in character. Its starting point is the familiar if now superseded partition of the world into western democracies (European, North American, Japanese or Australasian for the most part), the communist domain (largely central and eastern European) despite its now disintegrated condition, and the familiar 'third world'.

The West

What kinds of political corruption most relevant to the interests of geographers occur in the western democracies? Several areas at once stand out: the awarding of contracts by national and local governments to supply goods and services across the board from everyday supplies to major public works; land-use planning, and zoning changes in particular; the payment of subsidies to industry and perhaps especially to agriculture; a cluster of activities known as 'vice': gambling in its illegal and/or controlled aspects; prostitution and pornography; alcohol and other drugs (in each case mainly because of the problem of regulation); and thus law enforcement in general although a few areas, customs and welfare, are conspicuously vulnerable. These five major elements characterise rather than distinguish the western democracies: they are for the most part present elsewhere and it is interesting to note that the most nearly peculiarly western among them move outwards as opportunity arises. Land-use planning is weak or non-existent in much of the third world, but as it arrives so too does corruption, well documented in this context in Singapore (*FEER*, 29 January 1987) and Malaysia (*FEER*, 2 April 1987). In concrete terms this western corruption means manufacturers, wholesalers and contractors bribing public servants; land developers bribing councillors and planners (or conspicuously well represented in local government themselves); industrialists and farmers in consort with civil servants to obtain payments they are not entitled to; and pimps, prostitutes, drug dealers and bookmakers subverting police and judiciary. This is not to argue the exhaustiveness of the list nor of course that every such transaction in these areas is corrupt. In most of the democracies for most of the time the proportion is very small: some of the exceptions are regional, the French Riviera cities have a notably dubious reputation portrayed in the case of Nice by no less a figure than Graham Greene (Greene, 1982) for example; others are temporal, corruption usually expanding in times of war and scarcity. More typically town and country planning in Britain is locally and intermittently rather than thoroughly corrupt, corrupt enough to make a difference, but (for various reasons) not so corrupt that the issue has received much mention in scholarly literature, although particular incidents - not necessarily the fundamentally most significant - are extensively reported in the local and occasionally the national media. Gardiner and Lyman (1978) provide a particularly interesting account in the United States in the 1970s. More deep seated corruption appears to characterise a few countries: Japan, where the phrase 'structural corruption' signifies the close association of commercial, political and bureaucratic interests (Murata, 1979, 217-9); Italy, where the extent of corruption well beyond its traditional albeit distortedly viewed stronghold in the Mafia, the Mezzogiorno and public works has recently become evident; endemic corruption in some Australian states and cities. What is no longer or only exceptionally (and often geographically marginally) found in these countries also deserves comment: electoral corruption, now strictly monitored and much diminished although traditionally a rich field of anecdote - 'bring out your dead', 'vote early - vote often' - has become confined to say Ulster and Corsica; the black market, less so the black economy, is the victim of affluence; petty corruption (of say postal officials) is insignificant rather than unknown; senior civil servants and judges are almost invariably honest though the same could not be said with such emphasis of legislators - but compare a century ago. There is in all these favourable perceptions a risk of complacency and deception (self and otherwise) but it is a risk not a certainty.

Communism

The communist world was (and in its vestiges remains) quite different. Firstly the state was into everything while by contrast individual enterprise, in business, in farming, in infrastructural and social provision was at least highly regulated and at the extremes completely abolished. Consequently some actions fall within the definition of political corruption in the communist world which would not do so in say India or Ireland. For example getting spare parts, in a factory or for tractors on a state farm, a notoriously fallible area of the command economies, when it proceeded by means of bribe or backhander to or from a state or party official, falls within our definition of political corruption: the comparable acts elsewhere are merely dishonest. The same is the case, albeit to a lesser extent, with queue jumping in the service sector, a commonplace on the basis of payment or family ties. Theft as a servant, a common but non-political offence in the west becomes political in the communist system when the employer from whom goods or time are stolen and tools 'borrowed' is so commonly the state. This component of a more extensive inbuilt ideological propensity towards corruption (Ginsburgs, 1989, 620-30) provides the framework within which all kinds of manifestations occurred.

Starting at the top there is evidence that in these countries the decision taking and implementing élite (formally and more narrowly the *nomenklatura*) abused their power, legal privileges included, for personal gain on a large scale. The gap between élite living standards and formal status and that of the bulk of the population was larger and more clearly defined than in the west, and it was a gap which the élite used its authority to expand. Djilas (1957, 82), having been part of such a system, goes so far as to assert the inevitability of the process and his argument applies to any totalitarian or authoritarian régime: 'the fact that the government and the party are identical with the state, and practically with the holding of all property, causes the Communist state to be one which corrupts'. The privileges of the élite were not themselves corrupt, however anomalous their role might seem to be in a reputedly and officially egalitarian system. But the ways in which they were used was. Access to foreign exchange and travel and thus to imported and/or scarce consumer goods commonly underpinned the black market; the decision taking power in e.g. housing and education was up for sale, a better flat, a university place; the legal privilege of building a country cottage could be abused in such respects as land-use zoning and preferential access to labour and materials. The already wealthy sought to enhance their position and conspicuous display of their success contributed to the system's downfall as popular opinion increasingly discerned and denounced the gap between communist theory and practice, the gulf between the lifestyles of themselves and their masters and mistresses. At this point it must also be noted, and in the context of the discussion to follow, that differences between various communist states in this as in other respects were substantial. The USSR, a less functional and also less culturally uniform country than East Germany, was manifestly more corrupt. In the case of North Korea the advent of corruption in what had apparently been an almost corruption free system has been viewed as a symptom of terminal decline rather than an intrinsic and long standing characterisation (*FEER*, 10 October 1996). Finally the capacity of the *nomenklatura* to survive and revive, while retaining its old ways, corruption included, has been noted (Reed, 1995).

It was not however merely at the elevated *nomenklatura* level that decisions and services were for sale. Communist régimes (and again authoritarian régimes in general) necessarily had an abundance of decision takers and gate keepers at all levels, needing and willing to sell what they controlled. Having something to sell, which something was as has been mentioned highly likely to be an asset of the state and in short supply, became an essential tool for survival or at least for a higher standard of living, and everyday life at all levels became very much a matter of trading such goods and services illegally obtained from the state. It follows that it was similarly important to have contacts among these decision takers and gate keepers (Tarkowski, 1981, 177) whether vertically within the hierarchy or horizontally across the community. The client-patron character of the situation is apparent.

This was then the second main dimension of communist corruption, based on the notorious inability, itself in part a function of corruption, of command economies satisfactorily to deliver goods and services. 'Scarcity is the father of corruption, and the cadre (*nomenklatura*) system its mother.' (Lesnik and Blanc, 1990, 78-9). Over and above the intrinsic illegality and politicisation of many such activities in a communist society there were several facets of corruption: the black economy was commonly a matter of skilled labourers providing services or of goods being obtained on a cash basis that were hard to get via official channels. Corruption and its opportunities were an incentive to officials to go on making them hard to get. Plumbing repairs, good quality clothing, and veterinary services provide three examples. Moreover the work was often done in the boss's time with his tools, the boss being the state. Officials were also bribed to turn a blind eye, to bend or not to notice rules and regulations. Corruption this undoubtedly was, but it was made so by the enormous extent of state involvement, as discussed early in this section, and it was an activity without which most people would have been worse off and a few might not have survived. Holmes (1993, 203-12) thus asserts the delivery and safety valve roles of corruption in the old USSR. It was not however a reliable, let alone equitable system, even when manifestly superior to the 'official alternative'. For one thing, as Morton (1980, 250) reports, it provided a paradise for the con man, or in his best example concerning key money for apartments an Astrakhan con woman. In western and third world societies it is not too difficult to imagine alternative paths to such ends. Under communism they were not even available for open discussion. The black - and often corrupt - sector was the sole alternative. The distinctions however were rarely clear: it was usually impossible to distinguish precisely within the whole apparatus of ways and means of coping with scarcity and shortage between the legitimate, the ingenious and the corrupt. This individual level of activity with its strong component of corruption is labelled by Feher, Heller and Marcus in *Dictatorship over Needs* (1983, 99), an interpretation of the communist dominion in post-war Eastern Europe, as the 'Second Economy'.

The same authors describe the day-to-day operation of the economy at the enterprise level, notoriously inflexible and overplanned, often short of vital inputs, and in which the uncertain connexion of supply and demand on the production side was often mediated by corruption, as the Third Economy. Not only official but also unofficial channels made up the production process. The practically successful enterprise manager used contacts, barter and bribes to get hold of things needed to keep production going but uncertainly available through the official system. Raw materials, the invariably scarce spare parts (Katsenelinboigen, 1977, 80), even food and clothing were thus obtained. In one Polish instance light bulbs were swapped for tights! (Tarkowski, 1981, 501). This was of course to break rules and plans, and corrupt inasmuch as backhanders, misuse of government property and nepotism lubricated the system. Corrupt this economy was, at least in part, but again corruption made it a going or at least a more going concern providing more goods and services than would otherwise be available.

Nomenklatura élites, black markets, day-to-day bribery by customers and officials have equivalents elsewhere, even though they were a conspicuous and central feature of communist rule. 'Without corruption communist society would doubtless receive a deathblow' wrote Lesnik and Blanc (1990, 62), moving towards recognition of one of its distinctive features. There is no doubt that corruption was often tolerated and accepted by these régimes not only because it kept things moving but because it might enhance official control: 'almost every Ivan could be brought before the authorities for corrupt practices' (Shtromas and Kaplan, 1988-89, vol 1, 126). And yet the phenomenon of corruption, while it served to enrich the few and in the form of offshore remittance of proceeds to weaken the economy, was probably most important as a survival mechanism for the many. This forces at least an initial review of the traditionally adverse judgement of corruption in such terms as functionality and morality, a critique evident in Islamic thought as early as the seventheenth century (Alatas, 1990, 4). The traditional if rather feeble and pejorative defence 'everyone does it' begins to carry conviction where formal alternatives to the official system are proscribed and that official system fails. Bok states an interesting parallel situation vis-à-vis lying: the distinction between the free loading liar and the liar whose deception is a strategy for survival in a corrupt society (1978, 23). It is in the whole political and social order and apparatus not the individual citizen that corruption resides and which thus stands condemned under communist rule. Judgements as to both the moral status and functionality of corruption also depend on the commentator's assessment of state legitimacy, or more broadly on our approval or disapproval of the system being subverted (Scott in Heidenheimer et al., 1989, 142). To the committed communist corruption in a communist state deserves the fully negative implications of the word; to those who view the state as legitimate only when it is concerned for more than itself, for social justice and social change, political corruption in the communist world has at least temporarily a peculiar yet also positive and functional role. This is an interpretation focused upon its demonstrably effective operation both as a means of immediate survival and in generating eventual change even as what was thought and hoped to be an ephemeral phenomenon has turned out to be more durable than expected.

The Third World

'La corruption et la prostitution, caracteristiques classiques des pays sous-developpés - corruption and prostitution, the classical characteristics of underdevelopment.' Thus wrote Dumont and Mazoyer (1969, 169), by no means unsympathetic and certainly not inexperienced observers at a time when such insight was rarely articulated. One suspects that they perceived a philosophical rather than merely coincidental connexion between the two. Now such an image of the third world, depressing as it is, is familiar, predictable, universal and longstanding. Alatas, a most experienced commentator with forty years experience, describes corruption as 'the most serious problem plaguing the developing societies', a view now widely held. It ought always to have been so: petty corruption was present in most colonial régimes as was something very similar in their indigenous precursors, inexact though it would be to call it corruption. Traditional rulers were in many areas feared for their propensity to demand goods and services from their subjects, irregularly and intermittently and on a scale beyond what might be defended in terms of tradition or need. This ancestor of modern corruption was every bit as nasty for the recipient. The traditional citizen solution, to distance himself or herself from state and government both geographically and metaphorically is not without lasting significance. Grand corruption was not unknown in some colonial empires and at some periods, eighteenth century India for example, but in the larger European empires and at the height of their powers there was rather a strong tradition of expatriate bureaucratic honesty. There are remnants of the tradition, in the judiciary especially and of course in individuals, but a realistic overview of the third world sadly recognises the increasing extent of corruption in most states since independence. In a few such countries corruption is the system; widely it is central to the system; and the few exceptions, Botswana (Charlton, 1990) for example has been largely corruption free, are more often regarded as anomalies than as grounds for calling that centrality into question.

Corruption is evident in almost every branch of government in almost every third world country, in appointments to and promotions within the public service, in awarding contracts (and scholarships), in law enforcement, in economic planning, in the regulation of commercial activity by licences, and in day-to-day interaction between citizen and government. Writing of Brazil in 1992 Geddes and Neto (646) list as typical forms of corruption (on a rather strict definition) overpricing, 'speed money', illegal political donations, choice among tenderers, advance information, commissions on contracts, manipulation of regulation. The list does not come across as distinctively Brazilian. The four prevalent forms of corruption in present day China are listed by Wing Lo (1993, 46-8) as bribery of officials, misappropriation by officials, bureaucratic involvement in the black market, and favouritism/nepotism. From a different perspective LeVine (1975, 97) describes how departure from Ghana in the early 1970s involved nine requests for bribes (in an operation which took 13 days, 26 visits to Accra, 55 documents and 87 officials). The connexion of corruption with bureaucratisation is at once evident. The third world bureaucrat is in an especially strong position when as is so often the case, levels of illiteracy are high and thus access to information by the population at large is difficult. Morell and Samudavanijah (1981, 223) discuss an instance in Thailand's land rent control programme in the mid 1970s. Corruption has also been invoked to explain the typically low rate of return on aid investment in the third world, so large a proportion never reaching its destination. Certain departments are recognised as having either an especially lucrative or central role. Thus Mèdard comments on customs departments (1986, 123) and evidence from Indonesia in the 1980s supports this view (*FEER*, 25 April 1985). In this case the estimated annual value of bribes was $200 million, about one per cent of the country's foreign trade. Its essential basis was the department's ability to delay, and the extreme political influence of particular firms within the bureaucracy in general and on the waterfront. This served to make both corruption and its investigation complex. So lucrative was the situation that even a tea boy's job changed hands for $1000. As an attempted solution control was handed over to a Swiss surveillance firm even though it was believed that in paying for itself this measure would also lead to an increase in physical smuggling. Wade's (1984) study of the PWD (Public Works Department - Plunder Without Danger!) in India ranks positions in terms of 'profitability' and noted spatial variation in the irrigation context: an assistant engineer's post was worth more on the plains (the retail end) than in the hills (the production end). Interestingly where Wade has been able to show that irrigation is in India an area of endemic corruption, Bretton (1973, 238) notes that it is an area where opportunities are least in Africa. The structure of third world corruption evidently varies from place to place. Variability may occur over time and space: revenue departments are much more lucrative when land reform is on the agenda than when it is not. Education department posts are by comparison unrewarding but as Mèdard (1986, 123) argues crucial in that when it succumbs all is lost. Substantial bribes were sometimes paid to obtain lucrative government posts in northern Burma as the China trade opened up in the mid 1980s (Steinberg, 1990, 594). Finally the peculiar importance of police corruption should be noted. It is however appropriate to note at this point that the third world provides abundant examples of the difficulty of disentangling the separate roles of corruption, inefficiency and incompetence, in the case of forest revenue in Indonesia for example (Hill, 1994, 76). Kummer however convincingly demonstrates the role of corruption in the manipulation of forestry statistics in the Philippines since 1945 (Kummer, 1995). More generally the role of corruption in the relationship between forestry and logging companies and third world governments is receiving more and more publicity not least because of the environmental consequences of ill planned or unregulated felling (*The Press*, 13 September 1996).

Again what has happened can be summarised as an élite takeover, an élite of civil servants, politicians - the equivalent of the *nomenklatura* - as well as businessmen, agents and fixers. The élites in turn may be closely connected to external interests: third world corruption is only partially home grown and as Bretton observes much Western criticism smacks of hyprocisy (Bretton, 1973, 122). Thus French business interests had a central role in corruption in Gabon in the early 1970s (Bretton, 1973, 129). In a few cases the history of this takeover, which often takes the form of a new élite ousting an old, has been traced in detail, by LeVine (1975, 17-18) in Ghana for example who notes the close links between the rise of corruption, the role of state corporations and marketing boards and the financial needs of newly important political parties. In the more severe cases the decision takers, the apparatus of government and party and hangers on, become more concerned with the rewards of corruption than with legitimate activity. What and who and how much it will pay becomes the central criterion rather than one among several for decision taking. Corruption is no longer something 'on the side'; it has become the central political activity. At this point parallels between communist states and the third world situation again begin to emerge, an unsurprising situation in not dissimilarly authoritarian régimes.

The antecedents of this corruption require at this stage no more than brief comment. The extortionate character of some pre-colonial governments has been mentioned. Alongside the virtues of colonial rule in this context must also be mentioned the creation of an effective bureaucracy, traditionally and politically seen as an apparatus of colonial repression (but which might yet provide a decently paid job!) rather than an instrument for development. Expansion, often nepotistic, of the administrative machine before and even more after independence has also been blamed together with structural economic changes such as the creation of marketing boards and other para-statal organisations - the Cocoa Purchasing Company in Ghana in the early 1950s is a well documented case (Fitch and Oppenheimer, 1966, 48-52) - and the use of import and export controls. Not all old élites were eliminated in the process of independence; not all the élites which gained that independence, lawyers and teachers conspicuous among them, secured a permanent place; the influence of the business community waxes and wanes. However LeVine (1975, 62-4), from experience in Ghana, suggested that old established politicians were often the most corrupt. The post-independence period has characteristically seen the army, traditionally apolitical and cosmetically anti corrupt, join and even dominate the élites. The situation is appropriately described as one of competition between overlapping élites, similarly corrupt, for office and its spoils; and equally cogently as the interaction of the little man's need for a place in the sun and a share of his country's resources and the upwardly mobile class's desire for power and wealth. In Marxist terms this situation has been viewed by Gould (1980, 122) as the bureaucratic seizure of the function of 'reproducing the capitalist mode of production', and seen as central to Zaire's underdevelopment.

Two consequences of the extent of third world corruption deserve passing preliminary comment. Wealth so gained is often conspicuously displayed but even more often transferred offshore; it rarely goes into productive investment and rarely in forms which aid local economic and social development. There is reason to believe that this offshore wealth transfer is a major element in the economic problems of some third world countries. President Mobutu of Zaire had $5 billion in Swiss bank accounts in the mid 1980s, and the element of IMF proposed reforms which he most strongly resisted was the abolition of corrupt para-statal organisations from which the wider élite of his supporters gained its illicit incomes (Walton and Seddon, 1994, 159-60). The Marcos fortune, in US real estate and again Swiss bank accounts, amounted at the time of his overthrow to about $15 billion (Quah, 1988, 86), half or more of the Philippines' national debt. In a few exceptional cases however the inflow of funds into third world countries is at the heart of corruption: this in the view of an anonymous friend is the case in Western Samoa where in the absence of remittances there would be little cash to fund the process. Secondly corruption in these countries is a much greater part of the whole process of government and politics than in the western and for the most part the communist worlds, more of an individual and collective burden. Bretton suggests that the absence of constraints (and thus the scale of the phenomenon) is the sole essential difference between African and European or North American corruption (Bretton, 1973, 129). The geographical consequences are larger, more things misplaced, greater uncertainties of outcome, greater inefficiencies (not least as nepotism is probably at its highest here), and an intimate association of greater complexity and lesser competence. In lists of kinds of corruption present in the third world what becomes apparent on empirical enquiry is that scale and status more than method or motive are what justifies a separate consideration.

Conclusions

This brief overview began on the basis of a familiar if now out of date world model. Such a bare outline at once suggests that in the corruption context two worlds are better than three, that the communist and third worlds have much in common which distinguishes them from the western democracies so clearly that their separate consideration is unhelpful. The parasitic élite, the role of corruption in everyday survival, its contribution to economic and political malaise, and its very size are the four common pillars. Revel (1987) in particular gives support to this as the fundamental distinction: a western world where corruption operates modestly in a framework where business and government cooperate, especially where the state has centralist or interventionist tendencies; a totalitarian world, whether left or right but especially if it has collectivist tendencies, with a predilection for the kinds of corruption summarised above. Most generally he asserts: 'corruption increases in inverse proportion to democracy' (1987, 38). He does however recognise one essential distinction: in the third world corruption prevents economy and society from working (but again with some qualification required at the personal level); in communist states corruption prevented the economy from seizing up. The communist countries had economies, and perhaps social structures, unworkable both in principle and in practice as well as a political system inhibiting change. In the third world the alternatives exist, certainly in principle and even occasionally or intermittently in practice. Ward (1989, 16) makes the point that evaluations of the goodness or badness of corruption are necessarily comparative, and comparative of the realistic possibilities not merely of ideal impossibilities. Without corruption and despite its role in the demise of such régimes communism might have collapsed sooner and more dramatically, perhaps more violently: without corruption most third world countries would be more prosperous and that modest prosperity would be more evenly and equitably distributed even within the unfair framework of the present international economy. The role of scarcity in both can be recognised: political corruption can be described as 'a system of scarcity in which the vulnerable seek protection and thus regenerate the links of dependency and patronage' (Waterbury, 1973, 555). In each case Klitgaard's assertion that 'getting round bad laws' (1988, 190-1) is not harmful applies, and links this initial discussion to the issues of functionality and disfunctionality, morality and immorality to be returned to later. A second important distinction is made by the economists Schleifer and Vishny (1993, 608) between the relatively free entry into corruption typical of the third world and the relatively hard to join systems of the more developed world, exemplified in their view by the USA, USSR and East Asia. They explain the grander scale and greater damage of third world corruption on this basis.

One final distinction deserves comment: men are usually but not always (Monteiro, 1966, 62) seen as the driving agents and direct practitioners of corruption especially in the third world. In Klitgaard's phrase: 'it is the men who are wasting Africa's money' (1991, 173). But where women are in power no evidence exists to suggest that there is less corruption even though feminist geographers will argue with some justification that women politicians' *modus operandi* is not of their own choosing. Women do however occupy a distinctive place in other ways. They are often the recipients of the lavish expenditure so typical of corruption in whatever area. An evident and worldwide taste for pretty girls has led to the exposure of a number of remarkably corrupt legislators and officials. Where corruption is a matter of day-to-day survival then women in their role of domestic managers are necessarily engaged in petty corruption on an extensive scale.

Basic description of this kind cries out for examples even though they must be unrepresentative and uncertain. If they are spectacular they are exceptional and if they are dull they may be judged unimportant. What follows in the next chapter is a non-random sample, a discussion in more detail of what corruption actually is.

Notes

1. Acton was writing in 1887 expressing extreme hostility to the view that 'people in authority are not to be snubbed or sneezed at from our pinnacle of conscious rectitude' (Acton, 1956, 335) in the context of criticism of articles on the history of the Papacy which he had reviewed for *English Historical Review*. In Acton's opinion we should expect the same, perhaps higher, standards from those in authority as from anyone else. The next sentence after that on power is equally telling - 'Great men are almost always bad men' - and almost as frequently quoted.
2. I am grateful to Dr Marie Peters of the Department of History, University of Canterbury, for interpreting this phrase.

5 Case studies

Characterisation and description necessitate qualification and exemplification, even though each example is in some degree unrepresentative and in no sense normal. The spectacular and the well attested are most probably the misleading. What follows then is a non-random sample, a more detailed account of particular places and cases. The objective is to expose the reader to a diversity of more detailed accounts of political corruption *in situ* with a view to expanding his or her comprehension of subsequent systematisation.

The 'Guttersnipe' Fable[1]

An obvious risk in any study of corruption is that the spectacular will be overemphasised and the 'run of the mill' underexplored. The appropriate countermeasure might be to take an area more or less at random to examine the extent and character of its corruption. Such studies are neither easy nor commonplace but they can be constructed from raw materials to be found primarily in local newspapers on the basis of the work of investigative journalists. The record here is a patchy one, not all newspapers, local ones in particular, being of a mind to upset the local establishment, the inevitable result of such investigations. There are many exceptions but to write them up in detail is to risk legal action. The solution adopted here is simply to turn a real world situation into a fable which explores the same issues and insights.

Imagine, gentle reader, an investigative magazine *Guttersnipe*, published, somewhat improbably, in a country town where the editor, a skilled investigative journalist, had come to semi-retirement. His professional skills were to say the least considerable, both in the domain of investigation and of survival of attempts to prevent publication, having been practised in earlier years on such British newspapers with a taste for scandal as the *News of the World*. (And there did turn out to be a connexion between the editor's interests in natural history and his zeal to expose scandal.)

The area in which *Guttersnipe* operated comprised: a holiday and retirement resort which was also a minor fishing port, a resort which had fallen on hard times; nearby in a physically rather isolated district quarrying was of some importance; there is also a sizeable military and institutional presence; the administrative centre for the locality is separated from the resort by a range of hills whose traditional barrier role has been largely maintained; lastly the rural hinterlands remain agricultural but also with substantial residential (often retirement) development in many villages. In some ways the area is a microcosm of coastal England.

What did *Guttersnipe* discover when the stones were turned over? Two principal and several lesser areas of significant political corruption. The first of these concerned an area of saltmarsh behind a sea wall, an area with a long history of controversy and a present pattern of land-use embracing recreation, wildlife conservation - the editor's interest in natural history neatly provides a connexion - and controlled tipping. There is an unhappy, perhaps unavoidable, history of conflict between these uses, involving also neighbouring residential areas, most spectacularly manifest in a methane problem. What *Guttersnipe* was able to show was that the tip was being operated corruptly - as often appears to be the case worldwide, New Zealand included - to the ultimate and considerable benefit of a senior county official, sometimes to the extent of several thousand pounds a week. Corruption took such familiar forms as backhanders for machinery hire contracts and salvage rights and at a petty level misuse of the weighbridge, forms of corruption generally thought to be widespread in the refuse disposal business. (A recent student project revealed a local New Zealand example.) More serious however was the overloading, on the basis of bribes, of a carefully designed system for disposal of toxic wastes. Probably at least three times as much material as the system could handle was coming to the facility, from as far away as the Midlands (with implications for traffic and road safety). The sumps were regularly overflowing into wildlife conservation areas, destroying habitat and probably contributing to the methane problem. In brief bribery of officials, senior and junior, was preventing a well planned multiple use system in an environmentally sensitive area from working properly. (It should be also added that there was some suggestion of corruption of officials by the rival operators of recreational attractions at the beach end of the site.) Ironically the superior officer of the most corrupt official was paid off by him with confectionery from a nearby factory delivered for destruction at the tip as failing to meet the company's high standards! As a result of this case several officers and employees were dismissed or resigned but the long term effects of excessive dumping, which may not have ceased, continue.

The second major finding concerned residential development more or less throughout the area. Again the lynchpin of the investigation and perhaps of the 'system' as in the case already discussed was a relatively senior official, this time a planning officer, living well beyond his means, a circumstance so often central to the exposure of corruption. He was eventually dismissed but never brought to trial, possibly because political pressures were brought to bear. This second key element of the investigation was then a widespread allegation that 'certain people can build ... what they like', the certain people comprising a number of district councillors, certainly not all of them, and their friends, these latter often acting as their agents. The role of the planning officer, allegedly and presumably bribed, was to give permission for a zoning change, almost always from non-residential to residential. In general terms the typical allegation was of purchase of land without planning permission by an influential person, usually a councillor, or his agent, followed by a grant of planning permission and subsequent development of a kind previously not permitted and on the basis of a bribe or promise of promotion. Examples include a holiday camp where the owners, local councillors, got permission to build after the previous owner had on several occasions been refused, and a case where a councillor's son was able to build a bungalow across an ancient right of way. The complexity of ancient land laws in one locality allegedly facilitated corruption, illustrating the point that complication is one of the parents of corruption. Allegations have also been made of adjustment of the boundaries of development zones to the benefit of councillors and their friends owning and acquiring land just beyond the original boundaries. The basic consequence is that land development and land use reflects not the criteria and aims enshrined in planning documents and processes but wealth and influence and in some cases advance information. Secondly it should be noted that a small group became extremely wealthy on the basis of these transactions, their wealth going into property and lifestyle (both local and overseas), and ostentatious expenditure which often turned out to be their downfall. The features of this case are not unfamiliar elsewhere and will be discussed later: the vulnerability to corruption of any system where modestly paid officials and councillors take decisions whose impact is measured in hundreds of thousands of pounds is a world-wide phenomenon.

A number of other allegations also deserve mention. It is alleged that the developers responsible for demolition of a listed late Georgian theatre, a demolition permitted by the minister in the face of advice to the contrary both at the local and departmental level, were substantial donors to the ruling political party. Development plans for the harbour, a big financial burden on the council, are alleged consistently to favour recreational use and the local yacht club, of which many councillors and officials are members, over the fishing industry. In the currently important context of privatisation it is alleged that companies made up of councillors and former council employees have enjoyed privileged access to information, in the case of refuse disposal contracts for example. Further afield, in the north of the county, councillors and officials allegedly failed to declare a similar interest in the case of a nationally very controversial refuse tip. More generally there are allegations of the generous entertainment of planners by developers, of sale of assets to low bidders, of favour shown toward enterprises owned by councillors and even cabinet ministers.

Few of these allegations have led to court cases, largely because of the standards of proof required. Rather more have had such consequences as resignation or disciplinary measures or simply the at least temporary cessation of corrupt activity. A substantial core of these cases may be reasonably regarded as proven in which case political corruption has affected the geography of the region. An environmental problem, with both an immediate and a long term component, has been compounded with effects on wildlife, land-use and the adjacent residential area. A substantial amount of residential development has taken place where it would not have done so had the planning process been operated with honesty and consistency. In practice it is not possible to map the phenomenon as a whole, but particular cases can be isolated. Neither this county nor this locality have a particularly notorious reputation in this context. That was not and is not the basis of an investigation which owes a great deal to chance circumstances. There is no way of measuring the standing of this particular case in terms of average or typical conditions, but nor is there any reason to believe that it belongs at either extreme. The essential point of this example is to assert the significance of corruption as a dynamic of geographical change, not simply in a few spectacular instances, but almost certainly more widely. It is not a dynamic which many geographers have cared to consider. It is one which we neglect at our intellectual peril.

Burma and Thailand[2]

Third world corruption is endemic; it is also extremely variable. Similar contexts do not provide similar consequences. In this particular case two south-east Asian countries, Burma and Thailand, with much but not everything in common share a reputation for political corruption. Yet not only are the forms but also the consequences of that corruption substantially different not least in the fact that Burma is now a very poor country with an impoverished and until recently exceptionally stagnant economy, while Thailand, once at least as poor, is now a rapidly expanding economy with a fast rising standard of living. Where does corruption fit into that difference?

Both Burma and Thailand are south-east Asian countries with a powerful Buddhist tradition, and a generous resource endowment, not only of lands and forests but also in Burma's case of minerals. They both have a recent history of military rule but only in Burma is the army now in power. Overall resemblances notwithstanding there are also differences between the two. In brief, Burma underwent the colonial experience for more than a century and Thailand did not; Burma is ethnically the more diverse, with several traditionally powerful (mostly peripheral) minorities; during the last three decades Burma has experienced unusually continuous rule by a single military régime, and Thailand a series of coups and elections which have superficially at least emphasised political discontinuity. What has been the corruption experience of each country and how, if at all, does it relate to Thailand's 'success' and Burma's 'failure'?

Firstly Burma: corruption is nothing new (Taylor, 1987). Its ancestor was present in pre-colonial Burma in a monarch's service underpaid, often remunerated on a fee basis, and in which the distinction between public office and private gain was not clearly articulated (Furnivall, 1948, 171-2). The power of the state diminished markedly away from the centre, and in each avoidance of contact with officialdom was wisely and widely seen as a sensible course of action. Colonial Burma experienced corruption in varied ways (Furnivall, 1948, 172-8): the higher, alien and expert echelons of the civil service were generally honest but corruption was widespread at the lower levels in collection of land revenue and in municipal councils for example. Furnivall (1948, 112-3) reports that under legislation providing rural loans passed in 1884, the village headman took 5 per cent (which could equally be viewed as a fee for standing security), clerks a smaller amount, disbursing officers between 5 per cent and 30 per cent. Taylor (1987, 167) recounts the career in the 1920s and 1930s of a corrupt revenue surveyor, who survived an unsuccessful prosecution, to become a landowner, moneylender, and corruptible district councillor. The origins of like phenomena in Thailand cannot of course be traced back into the (non-existent) colonial experience. They are more exclusively home grown albeit possibly imitative.

At and for some time after independence Burma had the reputation of being not particularly corrupt as well as that of being a promising candidate for development. It was indeed and despite wartime devastation one of the wealthier and more cosmopolitan countries of immediately post-war south-east Asia. Now it is both very poor, an LDC (Least Developed Country) since 1987, and very corrupt (Steinberg, 1991, 738). What happened? The evident datum for any discussion of corruption in modern Burma must be the military coup of 1962, not because its leaders were themselves then especially corrupt (Ahmad and Crouch, 1986, 6), but because they introduced policies which fostered corruption in a variety of forms, a corruption in which they themselves were eventually much involved (Perry, 1993). Their 'Burmese Way to Socialism' envisaged and attempted what its name implies in a very bureaucratic and extremely autarchic form. The resultant Burmese command economy declined, eventually collapsed, under a burden of detailed regulations not so much bad in themselves or their intentions, as in their quantity and their mode of execution. Coupled with the much publicised attempt at a huge reduction in contact with the rest of the world, not only official and commercial but also cultural and personal, the implementation of the Burmese Way inevitably fostered an increase in various forms of corruption. Than and Tan (1990, 280-1) refer to: 'deep corruption that developed during the quarter century when the Burmese Way to Socialism prevailed (which) can only be removed by freeing civil servants and investors alike from the red tape of autarchic socialism'. As officialdom tried to control and regulate every aspect of economic and social life, often in ways which were manifestly impracticable, so corruption expanded its domain both as the citizen's practical solution to living under such conditions and as the official's means of lining his pocket - a very modestly provided pocket at the lowest levels - as he managed to 'trap the entrepreneur into paying a second salary' (Than and Tan, 1990, 281). Alongside this corruption there was the emergence of a parallel black economy, to meet as far as possible - and declining living standards denote that this was but incompletely achieved - the everyday real-world demands of the population. The corrupt basis of this economy was not its mere existence, illegal rather than corrupt, but the bribery of officials (Bandyopadhyay, 1987, 80) concerned for example with the rice trade, with urban markets in general, with transport, and with border controls (whether the borders were in Burmese or ethnic rebel hands), and the use by a small élite of purchasing and importing privileges to supply the black market. The black economy, eventually probably larger than its official counterpart, was dependent on illegal payments to public servants and military rulers to look the other way (Bandyopadhyay, 1987, 79-80). Likewise Burmese participation in the drug trade from the Golden Triangle depended on corrupting officialdom, both inside and in some cases outside Burma. A police inspector was offered $12700 a week for his cooperation (*FEER*, 9 June 1994). This particular but extensive corruption has been more and more central to the actual geography of production and exchange for the last three decades and might well be described as the corruption of need and opportunity. Its role was to 'deliver the goods' which the official system could not, but to do so at a much lower level than might be conceived under alternative systems of resource management not available under doctrinaire and powerfully entrenched army rule. The similarities with European communism are evident. The alternative to this survival or defensive corruption, as expressed in the black economies, was reversion to subsistence, a device probably equally important in the collapse of the Burmese economy. Not intrinsically corrupt the retreat into self-sufficiency, the withdrawal from the market place, notably by rice farmers often also required that officials be corruptly induced yet again to look the other way.

If the primary basis of the black economy was the need to find a way to survive in a bizarrely overregulated and isolated political economy, it was not as has been noted the only reason. An initially small and puritanical military élite - and it must be added their wives and families - soon seized the opportunity of privileged access to scarce goods to get rich via the black market (Steinberg, 1991, 173-4). The élite in Burma was always small by third world standards but its corrupt contribution to the black economy in this form should not be underestimated. What should be added however is that the privileged group remained small, and therefore its ostentatious use of corruptly gained wealth inside the country - and more importantly outside it - did not at first directly exacerbate the country's economic and political problems to any great extent. The same is not universally true and might not even stand up to close present day scrutiny in Burma.

The significantly corrupt activities of the ruling élite are to be found not only in the abuse of personal privilege but also in the abuse of decision taking powers for personal gain. Burma's isolation was never complete: there was always some trade and permission to trade (import and export licences) was commonly gained by means of an appropriately placed bribe. As Burma began in the 1980s to reopen to the world, at least for business, so opportunities for corruption increased, in such areas as oil exploration and most notoriously the teak trade, in the granting of concessions to Thai interests (*FEER*, 22 February 1991). This latter is of particular significance for at least four reasons (Perry, 1993): firstly the very high value of the commodity; secondly its location in frontier areas, notably along the Thai border where if ethnic revolt could be subdued wealthy overseas interests might most easily enter the trade and pay off Burmese soldiers and bureaucrats at a very high level; thirdly the consequential military implications of the corrupt sale of teak concessions; and fourthly because of the environmental implications of the kind of teak bonanza likely to result from the corrupt granting of licences to overseas interests in a situation of political uncertainty. Suffice it to say that the flow of funds from corruptly granted teak concessions has not only enriched the military rulers of Burma but has helped them gain a much stronger albeit not quite totally victorious position in their conflicts with ethnic rebels, and has generated damagingly rapid forest exploitation of uncertain long term consequence quite different to the conservation oriented exploitation systems developed by the British and continued as far as possible by some ethnic rebels. However since 1993 the élite is reported as giving up its teak interests, and abandoning its Thai friends and patrons in favour of a similar lucrative role in the politically and ecologically less sensitive offshore oil and gas industry (*FEER*, 22 July 1993).

It is then not unreasonable to suggest that in the absence of corruption, or more realistically with a great deal less of it, Burma and the geography of Burma would be rather different from what it is whether under a free market or a reasonable regulatory system. It is certainly possible, as I shall shortly proceed to do, to pinpoint particular differences. But it is necessary to recall that corruption is but one, and a generally underexplored, facet of the Burmese situation. Some of the others have been mentioned: the kind of economic and social policies that a different régime or régimes might have followed, the variety of possible outcomes of the ethnic conflicts bearing in mind the spatial concentration of resources, rice notably excepted, in these minority dominated areas. Effective secession, Burmese military rule, a reasonable compromise all provide different scenarios within which corruption might be variably present. It is certainly not impossible to imagine, unlikely as it appears in hindsight, a Burma in which the post independence years saw a solution to ethnic problems, a sensible development of the generous resource endowment with resultant rises in living standards, wise environmental policies, and a low level of corruption: in short a Burma in at least some ways more like Malaysia or Thailand. Finally the very modest quantity of scholarly and journalistic writing on Burma, for mainly practical reasons, though quality is often high, deserves comment as an obvious contrast with Thailand. These things having been said what has recent corruption done to Burma's geography?

Firstly under the military regime corruption affected every aspect of the rice trade but especially forced sales at low prices to the government (Mya Maung, 1991, 124, 126). Burma became a land of subsistence producers, apparently able to do little more than meet its own needs, and experiencing the green revolution on only a limited scale. Corruption in this area has been one among several conservative forces holding back methods and levels of production. It has retained this role as the government once more attempts a Green Revolution: villagers pay soldiers monthly fees to avoid being pressed into service as porters (*FEER*, 29 August 1996). Secondly corruption was both driving force and lubricant in setting up geographies of both production and exchange, internal and external, complementing the official and ineffective systems. These alternatives were in several senses corruption dependent, in getting supplies, in persuading officials to turn a blind eye. They were not and are not static geographies. Thus at the microscale the location of the principal black markets in the big cities has changed for various reasons, among them the corruptibility of key officials (Mya Maung, 1991, 134). At a different scale so too have patterns of cross-border trade, though in this context political and military factors have been more important. Patterns of resource exploitation, teak, fisheries, minerals have depended upon willingness to provide the necessary bribes, and have often run counter to more rational principles. New geographies have in turn generated distinctive and new patterns of corruption: as Mandalay boomed on the basis of expanding trade with China from the mid 1980s, so government jobs in that city became more lucrative and thus the subject of substantial bribes (Steinberg, 1990, 593-5).

Indirect results are necessarily more a matter for speculation rather than analysis. Inasmuch as corruption undoubtedly contributed to the impoverishment of Burma so it must be cited as a factor in the urban unrest of the late 1980s and thus to the policies of substantial urban reorganisation and ongoing repression carried out by the government. Bribery has also indirectly underpinned the relative success of the Burmese military against the ethnic insurgencies in recent years enabling the purchase of equipment formerly beyond the means of the Burmese military.

Finally there is the unanswerable question of the scale of the phenomenon. Firstly it is and has been widespread, the geographical sense of the word included. By the 1980s the black market was certainly greater than the official economy. Late in the 1980s it was believed that smuggled imports were worth about $200 million per year (Bandyopadhyay, 1987, 79-80), but other estimates have put the trade ten times as high (Steinberg, 1990, 589-92). For 1989-90 it was estimated that foreign firms seeking permission to invest paid about $50 million in bribes (Mya Maung, 1991, 287), and that almost every firm (most of them Thai) in the teak trade was corruptly involved with the régime. The nature of the evidence suggests caution, as do widely divergent estimates, but it also suggests that corruption is a major component of the life of Burma and thus of its geography - and of its wretched poverty and repression.

Thailand is also corrupt: it is also one of the world's more rapidly expanding economies. Why have things turned out so differently from Burma?

The first necessary task in answering the question posed in the preceding paragraph is briefly to outline some of the forms of corruption present in Thailand. Corruption is nothing new or exotic: it is, in principle, an old established and native tradition traceable back to the period when the bureaucracy was non-salaried and weakly regulated (Kato, 1987, 15-21). This may account for the traditional closeness of the business-bureaucracy connexion. The earlier years of the present system of government present fascinating examples: in 1948 it required seven bribes to ensure the transit by rail of a consignment of pigs from the north-east to the capital (Ray, 1972, 125-6). In contemporary terms a simple list of examples indicates the extent of corruption: purchase of rural land; tapioca and rice quotas and stocks; movement and promotion in the public service (an inspector's position in the police costs 3 million bahts, a director-general's 50 million); contracts in public works e.g. asphalt; timber concessions; the construction industry; car prices; trust companies; airport and airline operation; TV advertising; the fertilizer industry; port operation and development; leasing of bus routes (700000 bahts per route); military equipment purchases; child prostitution (Ockey, 1994). Evidently corruption is widespread and the list is not comprehensive.

Traditionally most important of the domains of corruption was its entrenchment in the bureaucracy, a bureaucracy with a strong centralist and authoritarian tradition in which the client's point of view was given only modest consideration (Sucharithanarugse, 1984, 157). In the 1970s the largest number of cases was reported from the Interior Ministry (Kato, 1987, 106) unsurprisingly so, given its size and its role as the centre of bureaucratic power over the regions in such contexts as regional development. Equally unsurprising is resistance to administrative decentralisation by those threatened by it (van der Meer, 1981, 150-1). In 1977 Neher observed the prevalence of corruption as business passed up and down the bureaucracy, obviously a significant matter in centre-province relations. Certainly corruption diminishes and distorts the flow of funds into regional projects and leads to higher input prices. Within rural areas to obtain land and resources nominally available under reform programmes a bribe may be required, and civil servants and their connections benefit from privileged information to pre-empt peasant rights. There is also evidence that rural development projects most amenable to corruption, typically the more technological, are preferred by bureaucrats for these reasons (van der Meer, 1981, 134). To summarise: corruption in the Thai bureaucracy favours core over periphery, town over country, powerful over impotent, rich over poor.

The second major facet of political corruption concerns the military, a powerful if not always in power force in Thai politics during the last half century. The most obvious, and geographically least significant element is the role of bribes in military contracts. What is bought is not what is needed but what provides the best kickbacks, reputedly of the order of $50 million to $100 million in three to four years in a senior post (*FEER*, 2 July 1992). The result is a military force equipped with an assortment of overpriced equipment not always suitable to its needs. Thailand is armed with six makes of tank and seven of combat aircraft (*FEER*, 2 July 1992). The military is also big in business especially in state owned business such as communications where similar practices have occurred as well as a more general rake-off of funds (*FEER*, 9 July 1992). To give one recent example it was corruption which allegedly kept Thai International out of the lucrative Bangkok-Phnom Penh air route in favour of military connected competitors (*FEER*, 17 September 1992 and 20 May 1993). The role of senior air officers *ex officio* on the Thai International board has been controversial (*FEER*, 9 July 1992). The military is strongly present and least subject to political control in the frontier areas where bribery has purchased its connivance or complicity in a number of illegal, usually trans-border, operations, and the drug trade and smuggling in general (McKinnon, 1992, 131-2). It should also be noted that the Thai military were well represented in the Burmese teak concessions of the last decade, most of which are just across the border and easily accessible from Thailand. Younger officers are less likely than older to be involved in corruption (Morrell and Samunandavijah, 1981, 279). In the context of the continuing debate and struggle between military and civilians for political power the periods when the latter is in control are marked by moves reducing the scope for military corruption, disbandment in October 1993 (*FEER*, 14 October 1993) of a specialist unit liaising with Khmer

Rouge for example. Conversely military coups have commonly and accurately alleged civilian corruption.

A third dimension of the phenomenon is its connexion with political parties and with factions within parties (Ockey, 1994). As these have become more significant in the competitive context alluded to above so they have, arguably of necessity, turned to business for funds, to such sectors as construction, transport, and the media not least but not solely to bribe voters. An optimistic view of the role of this kind of corruption is more tenable than in the two previous cases: it brings economically powerful but traditionally politically marginalised groups into contact with and gives them a stake in survival of civilian government. It may be the only way to get political parties going and most optimistically in the face of other third world experience may here turn out to be a transitional phase. (Other countries' experiences suggest this is unlikely.) It has not evidently inhibited economic growth but it must have added to costs. The new relatively corruption free container port of Laem Chabang turns round vessels in one third of the time taken at Keong Toey (Bangkok) and thus at much lower cost (*FEER*, 19 November 1992). It may however be that the combination of three major elements makes it especially difficult to bring corruption under control. The 1995 election returned to power a coalition party reputedly more corrupt than its predecessor, and that reputation and arguably reality contributed to its short period in office (*FEER*, 26 September and 3 October 1996).

Finally the international and environmental elements in the Thai situation require endorsement. Destruction of the country's forests, substantially by multinationals, and of those of its western neighbour has been significantly helped by political corruption (*SEAM*, March 1990). However the significance of the absence of any effective international regulatory régime also deserves comment in this context. As noted there have been downstream effects such as enhancing the military and political effectiveness of the Burmese régime. Likewise smuggling, especially of heroin but also in the wider sense, depends very much on the corruptibility of border officials and in turn is a force shaping economy, society and political conditions in border areas. In fairness the evidence suggests that corruption is diminishing along Thailand's borders, manifest in the shift of the drug trade to Burma's frontiers with China, Laos and indirectly via Cambodia (*FEER*, 18 March 1993).

Both Burma and Thailand are significantly corrupt: the significant difference however is not only the consequences - growth (for better and for worse) versus decay or even in the prognosis. Corruption is diminishing in Thailand at least on a long view even though it is both structurally and personally more public and more dispersed. The existence of the phenomenon is recognised and often acted upon. In Burma corruption affects all but is also part of a power structure concentrated in the hands of a very small secretive and essentially military group. In each country corruption has shaped geography and may be expected to continue to do so, but the case that it contains the seeds of its own decay is more plausibly arguable for Thailand than for Burma.

Mexico and Poland

Mexico, and Poland (especially under communist rule), exemplify the place of political corruption in countries where single party rule is formally in place over a long period of time, Mexico since the revolution of 1910 which gave its name to the ruling Institutional Revolutionary Party (PRI) and Poland from the end of World War Two until the late 1980s. Neither has been and Mexico is not a fully totalitarian society, but each was strongly authoritarian in its politics with the ruling party seeking to extend control over a wide range of situations, while in each case it possessed genuinely revolutionary antecedents, scarcely apparent however in recent decades.

In Mexico party and state have for most of this century practically coincided, hence the Institutional of the party's name. But a revolution institutionalised is a revolution tamed. Concessions to political pluralism, once almost unknown are now more common but they remain often faltering and uncertain. The process is not one of even and uninterrupted change. Throughout this period Mexico has been politically corrupt, an old established repertoire has been taken over, extended, transformed, and only occasionally diminished.

The literature abounds with references. Thus the Mexico section of *Latin America(n) Regional Reports* in 1992 and 1993 reports: corruption in the state agency for building workers' houses for sale on cheap credit (20 March 1992), corruption in approving both projects and occupiers; corruption in the offshore purchase of a new air traffic control system (20 May 1993); party corruption, 29 leading businessmen asked each to provide $25 million for the ruling party (22 April 1993); the procurator's office accused of drug trafficking, sale of information to criminals, 'lost' files, inflated pay rolls with some recipients turning up only to be paid (25 March 1993); army involvement, probably recent, in drug trafficking (Camp, 1992, 58-60).

Much Mexican corruption has a peculiarly blatant character, with at its apex the notorious wealth of presidents retiring after the single term of office which the law allows. Thus in 1943 one area was reported to be particularly glad that the ex-president was to be its new governor: 'he is already a rich man and therefore won't need to accept so much graft as our previous governors' (Whetton, 1948, 549). At present four or five ex-presidents are believed to be on the run in South America. Likewise the general ethos of the public service is and is generally assumed to be dishonest, and at such a level that a senior official has been known to acquire sufficient capital in six years to last a lifetime (Hansen, 1971, 179). 'Official positions, as in the old Hispanic-American tradition, are considered as ownership of a source of income' (Hansen, 1971, 166). 'Legitimacy is a saleable attribute' (Johnson, 1971, 4). This is certainly part of the heartland of Mexican political and bureaucratic life. It extends into most aspects of it, some already noted, and into land settlement, an area peculiarly central to the ruling PRI tradition. It is also evident in the trades unions on the basis of their control of access to jobs in such favoured areas as the oil industry (Story, 1986, 88). A few instances have very particular geographical consequences: corrupt acceptance of low-grade eggs for export to the USA, where they were rejected, brought about failures in the poultry industry in the Ensenada district (Ugalde, 1970, 93).

The centrality of land reform historically and philosophically (but emphatically not practically) to Mexico's revolution and its post-revolutionary politics has already been mentioned. The land was taken from the very small number of large owners and returned to tenant communities, the *ejido* system. Over the years the structural flaws in this system, very recently redressed, became apparent, problems with borrowing and selling and collective control which forced the peasant to choose between staying in poverty or abandoning countryside and interest in the land for the city. Throughout this process accusations of corruption abound (Ronfeldt, 1973) and the agrarian reform agency is usually deemed to be one where it is most firmly established within the Mexican government (Fox, 1992, 86). Bureaucrats and politicians combined to impoverish farmers in the period 1920-50 stimulating large scale and penurious out-migration (Johnson, 1971, 90-1). Extortion was used to delay and bribery to expedite land transfers. Rural credit agencies are and were corrupt (*FT*, 12 October 1989), as too are the processes of survey and processing of title (Ronfeldt, 1973). Corruptly induced evictions occur (*FT*, 25 October 1990). Water rights are corruptly obtained. Landowners bribe officials to prevent their taking action in instances of land aggregation. An especially well documented case (Johnson, 1971, 91-6) concerns the

1966 dispossession of a squatter settlement, which had been legalised in 1934, when the Department of Agricultural Affairs and Colonisation became aware of the property's mineral resources. Other current dimensions of agrarian corruption include: the 'crop loss industry', refusal by officials to report crop losses for insurance purposes in the absence of bribes (Fox, 1992, 99); officials withholding information on fertilizer rebates (while yet getting peasants to fill in the forms and pocketing the proceeds themselves) (Fox, 1992, 117). In brief corruption has stifled the implementation of a necessary albeit imperfectly conceived land reform programme and the overhaul of that programme. Mexico's agricultural crisis of massive subsidies, an inability to produce sufficient maize for local demand, and the underuse of the country's agricultural resource base all owe much to corruption.

An important regional study deserves mention at this stage (Goodman, 1974), important primarily because of its destructive relevance to the debate on the role of corruption in development and to the arguments developed from the late 1960s supporting a more favourable evaluation than had traditionally been the case. The study is of the *henequen* (a coarse fibre similar to sisal) industry in Yucatan and of the circumstances of its collapse (or euphemistically restructuring) in the 1960s, after two decades of prosperity, as synthetic substitutes entered the market. From 1912 the growing and processing sides of the industry had been highly regulated and were effectively in the controlling hands of large scale producers and processors who also dominated state politics and the higher echelons of the bureaucracy. In essence this group was able as the *henequen* industry collapsed to use both political influence and bribes to sell their processing plants to the government (at from two to ten times the realistic market price), thus transferring the cost of the industry's collapse to the government and to the small growers locked into a downward price spiral. The old élite had by corrupt means preserved its capital intact for investment in new enterprise, along with its political prestige and power. Moreover, as Goodman points out, money spent by the government in this way was money not available for appropriate agricultural diversification, for irrigation, cattle farming and fisheries, which would have opened the opportunities for widespread economic and social change. A few well placed bribes froze the economic geography of the region at a time when opportunities for change presented themselves enabling Goodman to launch a convincing attack on the functionalist apologia, an apologia and an attack returned to in a later chapter.

Communist Poland exemplifies, or exemplified as one of a family of states, the place of political corruption in another version of the one party state, a version explicitly socialist in its origins and its formal institutions but practically dependent for its operation on a high level of corruption. Because, primarily for ideological reasons, the Polish state (like most of its communist peers) managed and directed a very large part of the country's economic and social as well as political activity, so then many irregularities fall within our definition of political corruption which would not do so in a different political order. This at once tends to exaggerate corruption's role by comparison and thus a preliminary caution is called for. Nevertheless communist Poland was, or more exactly became, on any terms very corrupt.

As a starting point consider the part played by corruption in the downfall of Polish communism. It was no more than a secondary cause but not an insignificant one, the disapproval and disgust of the majority at activities of the politically powerful minority, not merely the official *nomenklatura* but others who realised that their position provided opportunity. Officially sanctioned privileges for the *nomenklatura* were hard enough to stomach in a nominally socialist society, hence perhaps Solidarity's egalitarian emphasis, but the central issue was the unsanctioned abuse of power, and not only by the *nomenklatura*, in such areas as provision of social services, building of second homes, and access to goods and services in short supply. No fewer than 12000 *nomenklatura* members were convicted of such offences in 1981 while Solidarity enjoyed a period of power (Taras, 1986, 61-2). The long term political and thus politico-geographical significance of this species of corruption has been disproportionate to its absolute practical role even though that should not be understated. If Holmes (1993, 42) is right it represents the failure of a deliberate strategy by the very top leadership to distract attention among the masses from its own shortcomings to those of the bureaucracy at large.

Both formal and informal élites also served as one of the components of the important black, parallel or second economy which has been estimated to account for 20 to 30 per cent of personal expenditure in Poland in the 1980s (Wedel, 1986, 37). These economies awkwardly straddle the boundary between the corrupt, the tolerated and the questionably legal, and the *nomenklatura* role in them was as a source of supply, having access, legal or otherwise, to goods and services to an extent well in excess of their personal needs and selling that excess - the corrupt act - to others and especially to wholesalers. Eventually by extension almost anyone who controlled access to a scarce commodity - scarcity is the mother of the black market - acted in a similarly corrupt fashion. 'Almost everyone has something to sell ... a relief package from abroad, a desk stolen from a workplace, or access to the state bureaucracy in charge of housing allocation' (Wedel, 1986, 36-7). A whole parallel geography, at every scale from local to national, is established on a corrupt basis to meet demand for consumer goods and services which the official system could not - or on some views deliberately would not - supply. It is probably the case that even operated fairly and skilfully the official system would have failed, but there is reason to believe that this kind of corruption is more a feature of the later than of the earlier years of communist rule, when revolutionary and ideological zeal had faltered and expectations and dissatisfactions, fanned by a degree of knowledge of what had been achieved in western Europe, were increasing.

As the system failed the individual consumer and as corruption provided if not cures then at least palliatives then something very similar happened at the larger scale. Decisions on the economy and on social services were extremely centralised and often based on limited and inaccurate local information and minimal formal local participation. State policy and local needs were often in direct contradiction be it in respect to provision of say housing (Brumberg, 1983, 49-50) or the manufacture of electrical equipment for example. The vertical channels for movement of ideas, information, goods and services and for deciding what went where often failed. Characteristically to get things done the local level relied on and bribed, albeit very modestly in material terms, its 'friends' at higher levels in the system to obtain preferential treatment. The bases of this 'friendship' were often in geography: of birth, of a period of service, of ownership of a country cottage in that particular community (Eisenstadt and Leonardhand, 1981, 178). The system was in many respects a wholesale version of the retail black market, a parallel and different economy established on a basis of irregular rewards though as has been mentioned these were materially modest, perhaps more significantly psychological, than in the case of the retail black market. This parallel economy operated up and down the political systems - recall the existence of a party as well as a state apparatus - and was augmented by horizontal links especially in business (Tarkowski, 1982, 501). The effective factory manager well aware of the fallibility of official sources of inputs and essentials did not simply bribe his superiors, he scoured the country via unofficial information channels - 'information is the most basic and valuable exchange commodity in Poland' (Wedel, 1986, 137) - to obtain what was needed to stay in business by a mixture of barter and bribe. Thus the corrupt connexions of the Polish economy made up not only an up and down geography deviant from the official line but also a hither and thither or even diagonal geography even more at odds with a plan and system which would not recognise its existence, role or potential (Siemienska and Tarkowski, 1980, 259-60). Evidently central places, especially in terms of material exchange, played a part in this geography quite different from that envisaged by official plans, a geography worth exploring while it is still well remembered.

Any discussion of corruption in communist Poland must emphasise this point, the absence of officially and ideologically acceptable alternatives to the official plan and system. Corruption, sometimes tolerated and as has been mentioned participated in at very high levels, underpinned provision of alternatives in a society where alternatives were legitimately unavailable for either implementation or open discussion. Corruption was an alternative to politics. (It should also be added that especially at the petty level its currency was peculiarly destructive: vodka (Hann, 1985, 90).) On this basis it is scarcely possible to view corruption as a whole in communist Poland (but not in present day Poland) in terms of either practical or moral condemnation. The most that can be said is to regret the necessity for so imperfect, inefficient and even inhumane an alternative, and to recognise the central role of formal and informal élites. In such circumstances some of the traditional analogies lose or change meaning - for example glue - although one commentator mentioned Poland's feudal past when exploring the strong links between corruption and patronage in the communist era (Tarkowski, 1983, 506). Whatever its antecedents the salient fact remains that under communist rule in Poland corruption created geographies, both durable and ephemeral, not intended by the official political apparatus yet highly expressive of real needs and aspirations, albeit imperfectly, in the only way open to the population at large.

Australia

Any visitor to Australia who reads newspapers or switches on radio or television will soon become aware that political corruption is a significant and ubiquitous issue. The fact that he or she would probably not have become so aware on the basis of the international media focuses attention on the principal location of the issue at state and municipal rather than federal level. Federal politics is rumbustiously aggressive rather than politically corrupt though the exceptions which have been explored, regulatory agencies of government, for example, generate interesting results (Braithwaite, Grabosky and Rickwood, 1986). By contrast some degree of corruption in state and local government can almost be taken for granted, and is endemic, albeit far from total. Corruption in state government is almost permanently up for display and dissection in the media. To this there are no exceptions but there is considerable variation: for the moment at least South Australia appears most honest while New South Wales, Queensland and West Australia have provided the most recent spectacular examples.

Corruption is in several senses a controversial issue in Australia. At one extreme a Marxist researcher views it as 'a necessarily endemic feature of our type of society' (Anon, 1981, 196) hinting at implicit comparison with other New World settler societies, and at the other a commentator claims that the assumption that that sort of thing does not go on here has inhibited investigation (*SMH*, 21 November 1984). In fairness it should be added that Australian scholarship and the media evidently take the matter seriously, more seriously than in say Britain or New Zealand. The latter provides an especially interesting comparison, of some explanatory power, in that complacent or not New Zealand, evidently less corrupt than Australia, does not have a state level of government, the level at which the phenomenon appears most distinctively significant across the Tasman Sea. Moreover New Zealand was never a penal settlement, and it was in the initial penal stage and its administration that corruption entered Australia.

Corruption in Australia is not then a creation of the 1970s and 1980s: the media of that period rediscovered an issue and activity which can be traced back to the start of European settlement. The New South Wales Corps of the first period of convict transportation enjoyed an especially evil repute in this respect. To this should be added land and railway speculation, especially in Victoria in the 1880s, at least on the majority view, and with durable geographical impacts: 'when the rails reached any particular point it was often found that syndicates of MPs and their associates had bought up land in advance' (Cannon, 1966, 29-30), the very MPs who had approved that line; 'money being borrowed by the state was finally flowing into the pockets of land profiteers (as vendors) many of them actually being members of the governments which were floating the huge loans' (Cannon, 1966, 29). Land scandals returned to plague Victoria a century later (Bottom, 1991, 44-6), and more generally are associated with areas of spectacular growth, coastal northern New South Wales for example (*SMH*, 15 February 1992). Lastly in this historic context the Mungana affair (Kennedy, 1978) of the 1920s, the sale of a worthless mine at an inflated price to the Queensland state government (whose cabinet included men with substantial shareholdings in the mine) deserves comment. It was not unique of its kind, except perhaps for controversy engendered, but it has been superbly written up and also provides an interesting example of flow-on effects out of all proportion to the initial event. At the time of its exposure as the great depression hit Australia, a key figure in the affair was about to present his first and probably very radical budget, as Federal Treasurer, a budget which may well have brought the ideas of Keynes and Roosevelt into play in the early rather than later stages of depression with potentially huge geographical consequences. A report on the affair was tabled five days before the budget and the Treasurer's career was over: his budget was never presented.

Contemporary Australia presents a diversity of forms: there is no distinctively Australian version - but there is the descriptive word 'rort'[3] - even though there is an association of particular kinds with particular states. Thus Western Australia in the 1980s became notorious for the close association between government and big business with big ideas - the classic corporate and one critic would add 'favouritist' state (O'Brien, 1988, 9) - which ideas eventually led to huge financial losses probably of between $A600 and 700 million and imprisonment of senior political figures (O'Brien, 1990, 118). New South Wales has by contrast a rather longer experience of a corpus of corruption linking the police (to the very highest level), the judiciary, drugs, sex, and the gambling industry. These had been highly regulated but in the late 1960s and early 1970s Sydney had 13 major illegal casinos paying out $A1.4 million annually in bribes whose recipients included the state prime minister (*SMH*, 17 October 1984; Steketee and Cockburn, 1986, 264). A routine 4 per cent take on public works contracts has also been alleged (Maiden, 1991, 16-17). A significant proportion of Sydney municipalities in the 1950s and 1960s were 'pervasively corrupt' (Parker, 1978, 302). Coastal land development in the north of the state has been linked to party donations (Temby, 1990, 146). It should be noted however that the NSW Independent Commission on Corruption (Temby, 1990) has been notably effective since its establishment in 1988 as a reaction to reality and reputation. However police corruption has once more re-emerged as an important issue in 1995. Trade union corruption has been especially associated with the Melbourne waterfront, and was a very significant brake on the efficient operation of that industry. A Royal Commission which reported in great depth in 1984 demonstrated the importance of its links with gambling, drugs and big business, expressing the essentially organised and conspiratorial character of corruption (Royal

Commission ... Ship Painters and Dockers Union, 1984).[4] Corruption may be one reason why the operation of ports remains, by international standards, extremely costly.

Finally Queensland provided numerous instances of corruption in the 1980s, a corruption of which the most distinctive element is aptly described as cronyism - the network and labyrinth of personal often party centred connexions - and which received huge publicity not, I think, because it was the worst or most significant case but because of the eccentric and flamboyant character of its leading figure, Sir Joh Bjelke-Petersen. This is the reason why Queensland is the easiest state from which to provide concrete examples. Its essential roots were little different from those of many other states, prolonged periods of one party rule in a situation of bureaucratic subservience, the public service's occasional politicisation, and inhibited conformity to those constitutional conventions and traditions central to effective Westminster style legislatures, conformity inhibited by a dominance of executive power. The result however is that it is possible to list and comment upon a number of geographically significant cases from the Queensland of the 1970s and 1980s as reported by Coaldrake (1989). These include donations to the party machine by winning contractors for health (1983) and rail electrification (1988); state government aid - of about $10 million - to an area where a Bjelke-Petersen company had purchased land, aid in such forms as weirs, bridges, roads and schools; dairy quotas diverted in 1986 from Darling Downs to areas in south-east Queensland where party identities had industry links; sales of National Park land for development to East-West Airlines (chairman a prominent party member) without consultation or tender; overruling of an Agricultural Bank decision so as to favour a prominent party supporter; overruling of local government decisions in favour of developers with party connexions; decisions relating to container terminals and stevedoring contracts; a variety of routine 'rorts' in such areas as police interaction with the vice, gambling and drugs industries; sale or fast tracking of planning permission for prime land without tender or enquiry; favouritism in contracts including payment for work not done; allocation of irregular expenditures by ministers to incorrect categories to deceive auditors. This is a long list and a substantial geography, a Queensland different from what might have been not only in what was done - the whereabouts of dairying for example - but also of what could not be done because the money had gone elsewhere.

The redeeming feature in the Australian situation is that widespread and characteristically blunt exposure of the extent of political corruption during the last two decades has had some effect, not of course on the corruption generated geographies, but on structures and on individuals. A not uncommon, not irrational but perhaps overreactive response is illustrated by the experience of a cousin of mine while working as a consultant in the public works section in New South Wales. Offered a lift by a public servant (in the same broad sector) from Sydney to Lithgow he responded by offering to pay for a cup of tea at a stopping point. He was somewhat surprised when the public servant insisted on reporting the matter to his superior officer. There has been effective federal intervention, institutions such as ICAC (Independent Commission Against Corruption) have been created, official enquiries have been made and published, individuals have been imprisoned (at judiciary and cabinet level) and many more have lost face to the extent that their political future has vanished. Ironically one of these unfortunates floated the idea of corruption proofing of laws and regulations (Bottom, 1987, 107; *Bulletin*, 16 February 1988). Whether this trend represents a durable change or whether the Australian tradition of corruption is so profound that recent developments will prove ephemeral remains to be seen.

Italy

During the 1990s and especially in 1992 and 1993 Italy has featured prominently in the media in terms of corruption. Thus in March 1993 during one of the most active exposure periods London's *Financial Times* contained no fewer than 51 items, roughly two a day on the topic. It would equally be the case that most outside observers of Italy over several centuries and including Italophiles have known that Italy was a country where corruption was present and broadly condoned in government on a larger and more evident scale than in say the Low Countries or Scandinavia without apparently, and especially since 1945, inhibiting spectacular economic development.

This old established tradition and connexion deserves our attention not only because of its links with the present but in terms of intrinsic and conceptual interest. In popular discussion and folk lore Italian corruption is likely to be equated with Sicily's Mafia and kindred organisations in the peninsular south. There is no doubt that the Mafia has always sought, often successfully, to corrupt the political process, and in areas of particularly geographical interest such as water supply and communications, protected as it was by influential politicians. But corruption appears to have played second fiddle to violence and intimidation in what was always in essence a protection racket. Unfortunately Mafia is often the first word to spring to mind when corruption is mentioned. In fact it is too easy and too misleading a model to be widely adopted. Mafia (and for that matter Watergate) are in the corruption context incidents to recall not norms to apply or terms to employ.

The significance of the south in Italy's saga of political corruption derives not from the Mafia but from the fact that in the new Italy of the 1860s and 1870s, and ever since, there existed alliance and compromise between the economically dynamic north, with a relatively clean political administrative tradition but where the best energies went into business, and a much less developed, poorer and traditionally corrupt south whose talented men were disproportionately well represented in a government and administration centralised - at the behest of the north - in a capital city essentially southern, Rome. That persistent and convenient administrative and political geography (including its propensity to delayed decisions) laid the foundations for recent scandals. Until recently however many Italians viewed corruption as a southern phenomenon of little importance in the north and thus of little relevance to the dynamic sector of the economy. Thus Chubb and Vannicelli (1968, 145) interpret the phenomen as the nationalisation of an originally regional problem as government power has extended and broadened. However some of the most influential Italian scholars, in post-war years, at first denied the importance and suggested the exaggeration of political corruption in contemporary Italy (La Polambara, 1964, 295-6). All that can be said in their support is that the phenomenon has had its ups and downs, whereas the popular emphasis on the south as the homeland of corruption was at least rooted in history.

The reputed achievements of Mussolini - the proverbially prompt trains for example - rarely stand up to scrutiny. Elimination or reduction of corruption was not among them. The corporate fascist state might equally well be described as the crony state in which big business did well out of government and failed to deliver the goods. Massock, an American journalist who had lived in Italy for some years, noted in 1943, in the context of the dismal performance of the once highly regarded Italian Air Force, that 'the trouble was that the ministers and high ranking officers who knew what was going wrong with Italian aviation were getting rich on the graft and patronage that were the due of Fascists who know how to keep their mouths shut' (Massock, 1943, 244). What might have happened had Italy entered World War Two with the reality rather than the illusion of well equipped armed forces? In this context it may also be added that the extra cost element and burden of corruption in government contracts in inter-war Italy was rendered less apparent by the context of tariff protection and censorship which prevailed. This issue is however one which must be returned to.

The shattering of post-war Italy's complacency with regard to political corruption reaches its initial climax as has been noted in March 1993. Although corruption had been a matter for intermittent discussion for many years - thus there are six mentions in the *Financial Times* in 1988 concerning the Mafia and public sector contracts, prison building, health care, railway bed linen, and earthquake reconstruction (twice) - the climax begins in Milan in February 1992 when a Socialist Party functionary was caught redhanded - and admitted to it - with a £3200 bribe for a hospital contract (*FT*, 13/14 February 1993). It was a remarkable event in that Milan had always claimed, and this claim may have been widely believed, to have been clean. Very quickly the existence of corruption in a vast range of activities in Milan became evident: hospitals, the metro, stadiums, airports, theatres, refuse disposal, reconstruction work after floods and public works in general (*FT*, 8 May 1992). Corruption was to be found both in construction and in operation and in practically every activity where the private and public sectors interacted. Milan was not unique: it would evidently be very hard to find anywhere in Italy where this was not going on, and it can be traced back via occasional, if only occasional, references in scholarly literature, to at least the 1960s (Walston, 1988, 78). The probably much expanded version exposed in the 1990s was then at least a generation old and in some respects and localities a great deal older.

Most reports suggest that public works contracts carried a corrupt levy of 3-4 per cent (*FT*, 16 March 1993) and that there was also rigged and collusive tendering effectively raising the price further. For building permits, regional programmes and property development 6-8 per cent seems to have been the going rate (*FT*, 16 March 1993). An additional effect was to deter foreign firms from participation. As the exposure process continued it became evident that political corruption was evident on a much grander scale in the world of big business: the creation of the chemical multinational Enimont in the late 1980s may have created $280 million in bribes, paid to politicians and others - each of the main parties received $10 million - to enable one participant Montedison to be bought at about 30 per cent above market value (*NYT*, 27 July 1994). On such operations the kickbacks were relatively as well as absolutely larger than in more modest operations. It is clearly not universal: in the case of the $135 million Asti hospital contract it was the typical public works 3 per cent (*NYT*, 23 May 1994).

The most distinctive, and ultimately devastating, feature of the Italian situation was the link with the major political parties, the Communists albeit on a more modest scale. Italian political parties ran on bribes to take favourable decisions, and the law did not make it easy for them to do anything else. A 1975 estimate was that less than 15 per cent of the parties' finances were legitimate (Earle, 1975, 68-70). It was reported in March 1993 (*FT*, 12 March) that their collective illicit income exceeded £2 billion. A situation not unknown elsewhere, notably in Japan, takes an extreme form in Italy. It has also been misinterpreted and exaggerated as in the Montedison case where the party take was less than 10 per cent (*NYT*, 27 July 1994). In general there is good reason to believe that the percentage which in such cases passes into private hands, a commission on a commission so to speak, is often substantially understated (*FT*, 16 March 1993). Nevertheless corruption came to be viewed by Italians at large as the domain of parties and parliamentarians rather than of individuals and the public services, and the judges who were chief among the exposers of the situation became well supported popular heroes. At one stage six thousand political figures were under investigation (*NYT*, 9 May 1994), and there were several much publicised suicides as well as attempts to nobble the accusers. A former prime minister, Craxi, was sentenced in absentia in July 1994 and connexions with earlier scandals involving the Banco Ambrosiano and the Institute for the Works of Religion (Vatican Bank) have been noted (*NYT*, 17 October 1994).

The significant long term result has not simply been destroyed reputations, particular and collective, for only exceptionally had these been notably high. Rather there was a reordering of the political landscape, a new electoral system implemented in 1994, new political parties and new men some of whom have already been accused of corruption. The question of the future of Italy has been raised since among successful political parties is at least one, the Northern or Lombard League, dedicated to at least discussion of this issue. Simultaneously Italian neo-fascism has re-emerged as a serious political force. One further political consequence has been the articulation of arguments that continuance of the anti-corruption drive, for all its past merits, would be a destructive political force, depriving the country of talent and activity. An amnesty has been called for.

This call is reflected at the local level where hints of corruption may bring government to a standstill, in Milan for example (*FT*, 18 February 1993). Since ostentatious expenditure featured in the life style of several notoriously corrupt politicians it is unsurprising to read reports of hard times in areas especially linked with the *de luxe* economy, Capri for example (*NYT*, 8 October 1994). The fact that Italy is one of the richest countries in the world is however of wider importance in this context. Wealth and growth have been no safeguard against corruption, but nor has extensive corruption inhibited that growth though it may have inhibited its equitable distribution. But is this really so? Spectaculars such as Enimont aside corruption has typically laid a burden of at the very least 3 per cent and probably more generally of 8 to 10 per cent on a variety of activities where business and government have interacted. In all of this Italy did not get value for money - it could have done better. As was pointed out by a *Financial Times* journalist in March 1993 the approximately 4 per cent of GDP spent in Italy on transport infrastructure - roughly the European Community mean - does not provide Italy with the returns which it would have done and does elsewhere in Europe (*FT*, 2 March 1993).

Italy is then a country with a long history of corruption, a history in which the spectacular has often been emphasised over the substantial, and in which popular complacency was long a major ally of the participants. That may be read as a warning to similarly complacent liberal democracies. Whether they will witness an explosion of exposure and outrage followed by political changes so great that they may yet redraw the political, cultural and economic map remains to be seen.

Notes

1. This section is essentially a restatement of my article in *Applied Geography* (1994), 'Corruption and geography: a fable', pp. 291-3.
2. The study of corruption in Burma and Thailand is particularly readily and effectively pursued through the columns of the *Far Eastern Economic Review*.
3. The word is defined in the *Australian National Dictionary* (1988) as an 'act of fraud or sharp practice'. It is first recorded in 1919.
4. The Royal Commission, a joint federal and state operation, produced a vast body of publications, best explored via the *Australian National Bibliography*.

6 What causes political corruption: prerequisites

The causes of political corruption are a matter for both intellectual speculation and practical concern. If we understood the why and wherefore we could claim not only a major intellectual achievement but an advance in useful knowledge. No one enquirer can yet make such a claim impressive though the collective wisdom may be and despite the assertions of a few of the more monocausal accounts. Political corruption is invariably a complicated and composite phenomenon in this as in other respects, and simple explanations commonly collapse into the non-explanation of the wickedness of the world as an irreducible and inexplicable matter of fact. Ultimate inexplicability does not demand or justify unconditional surrender. There are things which can be said concerning the causes of political corruption which extend beyond the mysteries of individual behaviour. In broad terms we must firstly look at the apparent prerequisites, necessary but not sufficient conditions, at morality and behaviour and at government (bureaucracy in particular) in rather general terms. Secondly (in the next chapter) we must look at proximate causes, the mechanisms by which corruption is operationalised and which include, *inter alia*, poverty, social and economic change, class (whether or not seen through a Marxist lens), economics and conspiracy. These are of course to be viewed as connected rather than separate causes.

The idea of connected causes - an antidote to reductionism - is present in most list like accounts of the causes of corruption. Brabainti writing on bureaucratic corruption in 1962 lists twelve concerns (in no particular order): personal virtue, education, religion, colonialism, poverty, punitive codes, stage of development, environment, structure, transition, special training, and reflexion of society. There is a usefulness in the breadth, even the ambiguity, of such lists, but they are easily reduced. Hope (1987, 129-33) in the development context provides: absence of a civil service work ethic, economic weakness, leader behaviour, expanding role of the state, cultural norms, and weak opposing powers. At the other extreme Holmes for example (1993, 157-95) provides a very detailed analysis of the last years of Communist Europe and the USSR: cultural causes - traditional attitudes, weak respect for alien (especially colonial) legal codes, the colonial bureaucratic heritage, ethnic variations in attitudes to the state, levels of régime support in the population at or since seizure of power, a culture of expectations among officials and citizens, alcoholism; psychological causes - group and individual; and system related factors - the impact of modernisation leading to an 'ethical deficit', inequality and inequity generating both shortages and conspicuous consumption by the privileged, the economic system (deficiencies of central planning), the legal and political system (the absence of alternative career paths and of checks on government power, a party above the law, the *'nomenklatura'*). This comprehensive list ranges from the most general to the highly specific, alcohol abuse for example. Noonan (1984, 499) explains its increase in the last third of the nineteenth century in the USA as driven by: 'industrial expansion, increasing ... wealth, immigration by exploitable voters, (and) post-war relaxation of moral standards'. Finally Alatas (1990, 102) provides a simple matrix:

	individual	institutional	situational
long standing			
immediate			

This neatly structures the connexions and incorporates a time scale which incorporates not only duration but also momentum. Corruption may be driven by habit or tradition as well as by present circumstance.

Morality

All of these lists contain elements which assert the role of individual morality - or its defects - in producing political corruption. It is an indubitably central issue but it is also one which, accidentally or by design, can divert attention from thorough going investigation. 'Rotten apple' and 'bad egg' accounts of corruption, quintessentially focused on individuals' shortcomings, rarely stand up to scrutiny or satisfy as full accounts. They distract attention from the rest of the contents of the barrel, from the barrel's condition, and from the environment in which it resides. So much is this the case that such accounts invariably and instantly raise suspicions of a cover up and can rarely be regarded as serious evaluations. Some scholars argue that any focus on corruption as a moral issue inevitably compromises analysis in other ways, Waquet for example arguing that in the example with which his classic work is concerned, post-renaissance Florence, it will misinterpret 'what was in fact a permanent *coup d'état*' by bringing it down 'to the level of minor morality' (1991, 96). Arlin (1976, 66-7) argues that the usefulness of Nigeria's several official enquiries into corruption in the 1970s is similarly compromised. Ironically Waquet (194) eventually develops an idealistic rather than a structural analysis: what matters in his view is 'what the people concerned really felt' and he also more controversially asserts 'there is no relation between the constitution of a state and corruption' (12). This in some respects comes remarkably close to Alatas' position (1990, 149-50): 'unless the observer gains entry into the emotional world of the victims of corruption, he will not understand its nature'. Finally some even more obvious shortcomings of explanation in terms of individual morality demand comment: if individual morality and its shortcomings and variations were the fundamental cause then we might expect much less variation in corruption levels from place to place and a more random occurrence. Sin is scarcely a spatial variable.

Thank you! You know, that I would never dream of accepting if I didn't know that the phenomenon was global.

Laxman, *Times of India*

And yet when these essential caveats have been entered the fact remains that scholars looking at corruption feel they must use words such as greed, envy, cheat and steal, and that they accept that they are studying the willingness of individuals and groups to take advantage of their own strength and others' weaknesses. Without these there would be no corruption. Thus LeVine (1975, 4-5) writes of the central role of the *individual office holder* (his italics), Banfield of the 'amoral familist office holder' (1958, 94) extending the question from an individual to a collective base, and Rose-Ackermann notes that 'the personal moral beliefs of voters, politicians and bureaucrats play an essential role in modern democracy' (1978, 234). Sarassoro (1980, 26-38) writes of inexperience, temptation and dissatisfaction at the lower bureaucratic levels; of ambition, self-interest and money at the higher. Engels (1993, 16) asserts the ineffectiveness of appeals to morality when its absence is 'what makes corruption possible'. But all also share Alatas' (1990, 116) view that 'both the structure and the individual are necessary to the explanation'. Refocused at the level of society and structure the moral explanation loses sharpness and simplicity, but gains in understanding and conviction.

The consensus is then that the moral condition of society not simply of the individual is an appropriate level of prerequisite explanation for effective and searching analysis. In my experience this account of corruption will be put forward by educated citizens of corruption ridden countries, not themselves experts on corruption but often exposed to it, in such terms as the absence of any clear conception of government, let alone any benevolent view of its activities, among most citizens. A more formal statement comes from Chambliss in the North American context: 'it is not the goodness or the badness of the people that matters ... (they) were simply acting within the logic and values of America's political economy' (1978, 181-8). Lethbridge, concerning Hong Kong, writes: 'the volume and scale of corruption in a country is mainly determined by its general tone or standards and by the attitudes or values of its citizens' (1985, 214). A recent analysis of corruption in contemporary China places the 'crisis of values' upon its list of causes (Hao and Johnston, 1995, 128-30).

Africa appears as a frequent example of these issues often in terms of the inevitable failure of colonial rule to establish essential and durable connexions between ruler and ruled. Cockcroft (1990, 95) describes this as 'the absence of a sense of public good' - a phenomenon also often commented upon in the communist context - and Leys (Heidenheimer, 1989, 62) picks on this as a vital difference between contemporary Africa and the at least equally corrupt (but soon to be transformed) eighteenth century Britain. Mèdard (1986, 116) however makes the especially telling comment that popular opposition to corruption derives not from any sense of public interest but from that of personal injustice. The memorable subtitle of Bayart's (1989) book on African politics - 'belly politics' (*la politique du ventre*) - also emphasises the role of individual greed. Whatever power 'colonialism' ever had as an explanation of the role of political corruption in the third world is inevitably diminishing, and commonly now discounted by educated citizens of these countries as was the case as long ago as 1966 when Monteiro, an Indian, discussed and rejected this argument as well also as that which viewed corruption as but a necessary passing phase (Monteiro, 1966, 68-9).

These explanations evidently traverse dangerous ground, where accusations of colonialism, racism and bigoted paternalism may be encountered, but it remains ground which must be explored. Note too that differences in regional culture (a moral element included) have been invoked in accounts of the geography of political corruption in the USA and have not been criticised in the terms outlined above. Thus Amick (1976, 6-7) identifies five states with a relatively corruption free tradition: Utah (an obvious religious component), Virginia and North Carolina ('old aristocracy') and Maine and Vermont (vestigial New England puritanism - no longer evident throughout the region). It has also been observed that collective as well as individual morality may change quickly. What happened in nineteenth century Britain has been more thoroughly explored than explained. And its extent can be exaggerated. To cite two examples municipal gas undertakings (Garrard, 1988-9) and metropolitan road improvement (Doig, 1984, 70-2) in Victorian Britain were notoriously corrupt. By comparison many third world countries appear to have followed the reverse course: lofty and sincere pre-independence ideals have given way to the individual family or collective quest for material gain of which political corruption is often a key component. To use Garrigues' terminology special interests replace general interests (Garrigues, 1936, 12). Some would view this transformation as at the heart of the problem of persistent third world poverty, especially as its distinctive feature by comparison with what went before is its capture of the once honest higher ground of presidents and permanent secretaries.

A final element of the moral explanation calls for comment. Many of those accused of corruption will claim when caught 'everyone does it' or 'no one was hurt'. Likewise the view that most would seize the opportunities that come the way of the few is commonplace even though it runs counter to observable everyday behaviour. Discussion of the subject generally depresses our view of human nature! It may also generate action. As has been mentioned the conspicuous prevalence of corruption in Marxist Europe certainly contributed to political change in those countries. It has yet more recently had similar effects in Italy. On the other hand scepticism as to the role of corruption in third world coups where it so often features by name is well founded, and it is evident that official anti-corruption campaigns often possess a hidden agenda more significant than their apparent purpose (Holmes, 1993, 142).

To summarise moral considerations must be talked about first, but are not often and certainly not universally to be ranked first, among causes of political corruption. If all men and women were saints there would be no political corruption. As they are not so then the issue of the moral condition not only of individuals but of people, places, cultures and institutions arises. There is a perplexing and too rarely considered or explored political geography of honesty and principle as well as of its counterparts fraud, dishonesty, greed and graft.

Government

A second starting point follows quite simply from such considerations of the goodness and badness of governments and citizens and is likewise easy to ignore or misunderstand, that of the existence of set, public and orderly rules for the conduct of political business as opposed to its conduct along personal, informal, *ad hoc* or self seeking lines. In crude terms this is to place the blame for corruption on the existence of law and order, and more especially bureaucracy. (An almost equally crude response is to suggest that small government equals small corruption (*FEER*, 23 March 1995).) In van Klaveren's words: 'corruption is built on the underlying principle that people are subjected to the control of officials' (Heidenheimer et al., 1989, 55). The nature and status of that officialdom affects our concept of corruption: when public office, legislative, executive or judicial, could be bought as an investment or was a matter of personal allegiance then both doing the job and the concept of doing it corruptly differed from the same concepts applied to a modern bureaucracy. The rise of this latter kind of government has both sharpened and extended the concept of corruption, yet while opportunity has increased incidence has often diminished at least in the western democracies. This has not however been the case in the former colonies and dependencies where the argument that corruption is the offspring of the colonial experience and especially of its bureaucratic apparatus, increasingly viewed as a means of material personal advancement rather than a public service, is often advanced (*FEER*, 7 April 1995, 30). The general connexion is explored elsewhere but the narrow bureaucratic case collapses in the face of the evidence that colonial bureaucracies while not totally clean at the lowest levels were generally more so than their successors. It might even be argued that present corrupt systems have more in common with pre-colonial regimes which if not corrupt *strictu sensu* (for reasons outlined above) were not uncommonly notoriously even terrifyingly arbitrary and greedy.

Bureaucracy remains a matter for exploration here simply because without it there could be no corruption. Interestingly the possibility of political corruption (strictly defined) scarcely crops up in Weber's classic work on bureaucracy. As a complete account it is certainly a straw man. Its universal role is as context not cause, and it becomes the latter only when bureaucracy is degenerate - excessive size included - or perverted, a situation now so common that the very word bureaucracy is more likely to be understood in this pejorative than in its more traditional and exact sense. For predictable, public, orderly, expeditious process (all characteristics and innovations of pioneering modern bureaucracies) substitute uncertainty, unrealistic and unpublished rules, disorder, and delay. The possibilities are numerous: Calvert points out that 'corrupt officials have a vested interest in the proliferation of regulations' (1989, 203) and LeVine (1975, 39) quotes a Ghanaian's remark that public servants are experts in the complication of simplicity. When the House of Lords investigated European Community fraud in 1988-89 (House of Lords, 1988-89, paragraphs 58-62 and 64-74) it specifically cited the complexity and ineptitude of regulations governing export refunds and administrative controls. Malraux (Madsen, 1990, 200-2) exposed rule manipulation by civil servants as the core of corruption in French Indochina. Chambliss (1978, 211-2) described liquor licensing regulations so drafted as to permit any bar to be closed down at any time. Corruption resides not in the principle of bureaucracy but in its perversion.

The very apparatus of government may then be so designed or flawed as to invite or necessitate corruption. Thus most of Latin America has a legal tradition of complex written codes with their roots in Roman Law, roots probably now less important than accretions and momentum, and that complexity is one of the pillars of long standing and widespread corruption (Calvert, 1989, 205). In most general terms Common Law might be favourably compared with the Latin tradition in this respect. Recall however that in England Equity grew up to remedy the shortcomings, especially unfairness, of Common Law and in its turn became notoriously over complicated. A narrow focus on the legal and administrative system is however potentially unhelpful: a correspondent to the *Far Eastern Economic Review* on 18 June 1992 argues against such an approach and emphasises the need for 'fundamental rethinking of the nature of the state'.

A most forceful contemporary and influential presentation of this argument is de Soto's book *The Other Path: the invisible revolution in the Third World* (1989). Underdevelopment in Peru and traditional popular and corrupt strategies for coping with it are viewed and analysed as a response to a contemporary (but historically grounded) 'mercantilism' in which a bureaucratic and law ridden state regards 'redistribution' of national wealth as more important than its production or increase. (Redistribution here has a particular and slightly unusual meaning of the granting of monopolies and favoured status to a small and established élite.) De Soto thus connects an interesting set of 'class' arguments in this causal context, to be discussed shortly, with the bureaucratic explanation. It is also echoed in Tarkowski's (1988, 65) analysis of Poland in the 1980s. Finally the long standing argument that dictatorships or totalitarian political orders inevitably engender corruption deserves reiteration at this point in the case of Communist Central and Eastern Europe for example (Djilas, 1957, 82).

This is not however to exhaust the exploration of relationships between structure and corruption. Japan exemplifies, and in an extreme version, a once relatively common situation, the movement of senior public servants on (sometimes early) retirement into closely related private sector work where not only expertise, but also contacts and knowledge will be useful (Nester, 1990, 143). Such a situation is not intrinsically corrupt but is a seed bed for corruption (as well as for definitional discussion). In Japan it is usually seen as one of the bases of extensive corruption, traditionally but maybe no longer actually much less so in France where public-private sector moves (and vice versa) are commonplace (*The Times*, 11 July 1996, 10, 17). In Britain senior public servants and military officers may be banned from certain kinds of private sector work on retirement as a measure to inhibit corruption, a measure rather half heartedly applied and uncertainly effective (Theobald, 1990, 61).

Bureaucracy

Three particular features of bureaucracy stand out in the context of corruption, two of them as undoubted perversions, delay and complication, and the third as a specifically geographical element -

distance. The first of these is easily exemplified: de Soto's (133-4) (experimental) attempt to set up a small clothing factory in Peru involved eleven bureaucratic stages which took 289 days. Ten bribes were requested, two of which were inescapable if progress was to be made. Both corruption and the informal economy thrive in such circumstances, creating quite a different geography of retailing and small scale industry from what would exist if the official processes were followed - or if they were simpler. Payments made to circumvent such official procedures are often called 'speed money'. The effect is in fact quite the reverse for very soon the papers only move at all - and then slowly - if such payments are made. 'Speed money' for the few is a full stop for the many.

Complexity is evidently a close cousin of delay. Its role is simply stated by Reisman: 'the more prescriptions there are the more deviance there can be' (1979, 4). Rules and regulations often remain in force when they have become practically irrelevant, their origins and intentions forgotten (Perry, 1990, 203). In these circumstances the bribe is seen as the solution. However there are instances where complex rules are needed, building and safety standards for example, in which case the citizen is more likely to be the villain than is the politician planner or official whose culpability is rather a failure to demonstrate the benefits of such rules and to ensure that they are amended if there are none. Finally the close connexion between bureaucratic complexity (defensible or contrived) and bureaucratic confusion and incompetence deserves mention.

The question of distance in this bureaucratic context is not only the most complicated and controversial but also the most obviously geographical. Quite apart from the more strictly geographical interpretation however the question also arises of the distance between official and citizen. How necessary to honest and effective government is it that the citizen be kept at arms length? How risky, how wise are endeavours to humanise and strengthen the system by incorporating a citizen input, or at least listening to what he or she has to say, in the decision making process? In the more specifically geographical sense distance becomes a major component of bureaucratic geography and thus in turn of the structure of government. There is and has been here enormous variation. At first sight decentralisation of decision taking, the locus of corruption, seems to have been inevitable until almost instantaneous communication - the telegraph is probably the key invention - became possible. But Spain tried to run a most centralised empire in the sixteenth and seventeenth centuries, and while the centralist tradition in France peaked in the age of train and telegraph this was really the extension of an older tradition. The decentralisation of public procurement in France has been argued as a cause of its increased corruption as it exposed this activity to the corruption endemic in local government and moreover made corruption a more complex and diffuse target. Britain by contrast enjoyed a more truly local government as did its colonial subjects. In the latter case for reasons both practical and ideological the 'man in the district' enjoyed enormous power, inevitably with a discretionary element, and traditionally railed against a remote, ill informed, even malevolent capital city - a distant bureaucracy. But the question of the relationship between the centralisation or decentralisation of the government process and political corruption has no simple answer. The arguments are familiar: the preference of capital based politicians and officials for central control on grounds of consistency, economy and maybe the enforceability of policy, but also the risks of inadequate information, insensitivity to local views and inflexibility in special circumstances. The decentralist case turns these on their head: local knowledge, local opinion, speedy decision, the humanisation of relationships (Benson, 1978, 207) (an argument however also advanced in defence or explanation of corrupt 'machine politics') with the risk of things getting out of control and of an unduly cosy and over frequent relationship between officials, local politicians and citizens. A Nigerian commentator Olowu, quoted by Davidson (1992, 314), observes: 'the bane of local government in the Third World has been the overkill of central supervision rather than the chaos or corruption of independent existence'. (Similar arguments arise with respect to the frequency of transfer of officials.) Thus Furnivall (1948, 271) regarded differences in the mobility patterns of civil servants as one reason why the Dutch East Indies had been less corrupt than Burma. Some observers suggest that the matter is essentially superficial concerned with nothing more than the locus of corruption (Hao and Johnston, 1995, 121-36) and not with fundamental cause. Only occasionally are there what seem to be clear and unambiguous connexions, for example between extreme centralisation of decision taking in present day South Korea (*FEER*, 23 March 1995) and in Ghana in the 1970s (Arlin, 1976, 67) and a high level of corruption. The risk in this analysis is of return to an exaggerated focus on the morality and behaviour of individuals, officials and citizens. If it be allowed that there are several geographies of good government with often modest margins separating optimal from acceptable yet there are also more numerous systems whose attributes, geographical organisation among them, foster and facilitate the corruption of politics. Finally it must be recognised that not only national but international geographies are to be taken into account in an era when the role of international business and international activity such as aid is a more important component of corruption than was formerly the case (Clark, 1988, 123).

What then are the features which make some bureaucracies more corruptible than others? Geographical attributes may matter, an excess of local discretion for example, or the geographical separation of economic and political interests in New Jersey, as noted by Amick (1976, 7), when that state was infamously corrupt. But there is much else besides: Japan's structural corruption is shorthand for the close links (until recently culturally acceptable at least to the Japanese establishment) between civil servants, law makers and businessmen (some of whom have experience in more than one of these categories) in a political and social order which is highly competitive and in which status maintenance and gift giving are very important (Stockwin, 1975, 128-9). The prevalence of corruption is in such circumstances unsurprising. Liberal democracies where civil servants are appointed on the basis of education and competence - a central reform of the Civil Service in Victorian Britain - and enjoy an adequate and reliable salary and pension, and work within both a tradition and formal code regulating their interaction with the public have a good chance of getting non-corrupt government. In the third world and the communist states there are evident constraints on such possibilities, affordability, ideology (the leading role of the party shrinks the pool of talent), nepotism. Davidson (1992, 209) comments on the eventual merger of bureaucracy and clientelism in Africa, the need and pressure to indigenise - and less justifiably to expand - in the early years of independence, and a cultural climate which while it does not endorse corruption *per se* yet sees the holder of government office as universal provider for a very extended family. This list also incorporates some of the factors which explain the many instances where independence from colonial rule soon brought about a massive expansion of corruption from formerly constrained levels, and thus too a massive qualification if not quite outright dismissal of a simple 'colonial' explanation of corruption.

What is forever going on in this argument is that discussion of the bureaucratic element in corruption inevitably broadens out into a discussion of the quality and quantity of government. A government of good and well founded repute, effective in policy implementation, aware of limitations to what it can achieve, and open to public debate, criticism and eventual orderly replacement by its opponents is equipped with strong bulwarks against corruption but they are not bulwarks which can be instantaneously acquired. By contrast the Mexican type of situation of institutionalised one-party rule, a legalistic and centralist administrative tradition, a limited non-repeatable tenure of the highest office, and a long experience and reputation of dishonest government facilitates corruption and cannot be changed overnight. The connexion between continuous rule by one party and a propensity to political corruption even when the broad political context is democratic has often been commented upon. The weakness of political dialogue in such a situation was fundamental to the place of political corruption in post-war Italy. More generally a connexion between corruption and the funding needs of political parties has received frequent comment, in the case of Japan for example (MacDougall, 1988, 195; Curtis, 1988, 185). On a much narrower front Poulson's success has been ascribed to his ability - and presumably the established system's inability - to handle or to provide new structures to handle an increasing volume of technically innovative work (Gillard and Tomkinson, 1980, 44-5). In some cases attempts to be user friendly do not help. An Australian enquiry found corruption to be commonest in government regulatory agencies (concerned with consumer and corporate affairs) where the agency tried to combine the punitive and the cooperative approaches to its clients. 'Deterrence tends to corrupt and fraternal deterrence corrupts absolutely.' (Braithwaite, Grabosky and Rickwood, 1986, 184).

However as we explore government operations so too our concept of corruption changes and loses force and focus especially as we encounter incompetent and malevolent administrations which rouse our sympathy with the citizen. When as is so often the case even with the simple low level bribe, the motivation is to make an unjust or unworkable system fairer or more functional then the basic concept of corruption is called into question, a point dealt with elsewhere. This commonplace situation likewise underpins the important debate as to the functional or dysfunctional character of political corruption discussed in chapter nine.

Power

Acton's dictum evidently has a place in this discussion of bureaucracy and corruption as well as more generally, since bureaucracy is in essence the organisation and formalisation of power. Given the wide currency of the dictum it is very surprising that corruption features so little in discussions of political power. Acton was epigrammatic rather than original for the idea can be traced back at least as far as Calvin (Rogow and Lasswell, 1963, 6) and has perhaps been independently rediscovered, by Owusu (LeVine, 1975, 49-50) in post-colonial

Nigeria who sees a deep seated obsession with power as the base of that country's corruption and other ills. The assertion is both of a prerequisite and of more immediate cause, and its controversial and cryptic dimension has been commented upon. These comments testify to its capacity to make people think to which Bok (1984, 106) adds the useful rider that secrecy increases power - and thus corruption. In practical terms the dictum is often read as common sense advice to citizens, statesmen and political reformers - always keep in mind the possibility of corruption. (From this it is but a short step to the idea of corruption proofing, discussed elsewhere, a practical difficulty but a stimulating concept.) A much less often quoted if rather cryptic dictum of Acton linking corruption, centralisation and absolutism in many respects summarises any discussion which leads from a narrowly bureaucratic to a more widely governmental perspective: 'no power can so effectively resist the tendencies of centralisation, of corruption, and of absolutism, as that community which is the vastest that can be included in a state, which imposes on its members a consistent similarity of character, interest and opinion, and which arrests the action of the sovereign by the influence of a divided patriotism' (Acton, 1956, 159).

7 What causes political corruption: proximates

The preceding chapter looked at morality, bureaucracy, government and power not so much as immediate causes but as essential contexts for political corruption. These are the contexts which are the breeding grounds, but as several writers point out corruption is not accidental or coincidental or inevitable; it is the deliberate and decided outcome of particular decisions and purposes, of proximate causes as well as of wider contexts.

Poverty, inequality and scarcity

The most traditional and straightforward of these proximates is individual poverty, especially in the third world. Here even the lowest ranking civil servants have considerable power and prestige but are not necessarily well paid or reliably paid. This latter has also if less often been true at quite elevated levels. Lethbridge asserts that the key to corruption in imperial China was the low pay of district magistrates, a situation recognised in additional *yang lian* ('to nourish incorruption') allowances (1985, 11-14). Governor Mandel, an undoubtedly corrupt governor of Maryland in the 1970s, received a salary of only $25000 a year (Jacobs, 1984, 72): one US mayor is reported as having received as much each month from a single contractor (Barlow, 1993, 333). The most obvious limitation of this explanation must however at once be noted: well paid officials are no less likely to be corrupt than poorly paid ones. The 'second salary' extracted by the corrupt official is not invariably a matter of necessity (Than and Tan, 1990, 261). It has also been widely observed that corrupt officials rarely change their habits when they move into well paid posts: they simply put up the price. A very common element in this account is the strength and extent, again especially but not exclusively in the third world, of family obligations and expectations. The civil servant is a source not only of pride but of provision, of loans, school fees, medical expenses, employment. He or she is a reputedly wealthy individual in a poor society. In some cases, the Pacific Islands for example, cultural traditions of conspicuous generosity and ostentatious wealth display

83

compound the problem. Hao and Johnston (1995, 134) assert the importance of personal ties within Confucian culture as a cause of corruption. A further dimension is suggested by Arlin (1976, 67) in the West African context, 'imitation of corrupt superiors by their subordinates'.

By comparison with the third world civil servants in Europe, North America and Australasia appear to enjoy secure well paid jobs with modest social and family obligations. The factuality of this account may be contested: public servants may be poorly paid, public service restructuring, as during the last decade in New Zealand, may reduce job security. I would suspect that family pressures for financial help in crisis situations are commonly very much understated in the western tradition of reticence and secrecy about money matters. Finally the status of the civil service in the United States in its relationship to party nominated officials has sometimes been cited as a cause of corruption.

Our aim thus far has been to qualify and extend an oversimple and limited but undoubtedly relevant explanation. Poverty is an important part of the explanation of one important category of corruption. Poverty is however a more widely significant issue here than the well known account of third world petty corruption in these terms. Above all it needs to be restated in terms of inequality and scarcity (Lesnik and Blanc, 1990, 64), issues central to the wider understanding of political corruption. Whatever its immediate and superficial aims corruption depends upon, sustains and accentuates (Hao and Johnston, 1995, 145-6) inequality, spatial inequalities included, even as social, economic and political inequalities provide its occasions and opportunities. Its role as a conservative social force maintaining or enhancing an unequal *status quo* even while making survival possible for its victims has rarely been challenged whatever its secondary role in providing a ladder of upward individual mobility: thus LeVine (1975, 19) characterised political corruption in Ghana as the fleecing of the peasantry for the benefit of the emerging middle class. The implications of this situation may engender a profound pessimism: as Holmes (1993, 49) remarks 'if it is the case that one of the many factors leading to corruption is perception of inequalities and/or shortages then it is very difficult ... to envisage a situation, in the real world in which such perceptions could be fully eradicated'.

The idea of inequality extends the debate beyond the inadequate and unreliable pay of civil servants in many third world countries. A classic instance is land-use zoning in the western democracies, the process whereby, in Britain for example, officials and councillors whose salaries and allowances are measured in thousands of pounds take decisions which may augment - very rarely lessen - land values by millions. The same situation exists in the awarding of contracts. Corruption ensues and is I suspect more often under than overstated. Land-use planning in Britain is probably more corrupt than it appears, not totally, just more. But to what extent it is impossible to say. There is moreover no obvious solution. Someone somewhere must decide and cannot possibly be paid on the same scale as that of the decisions. In any case all evidence suggests that this would not guarantee honesty. We are forced back to reliance on individual integrity but we should also recognise the better and the worse, the more and the less corruption prone planning and purchasing systems.

The Guardian, 16. 11.1994

These unequal relationships are equally present in such concepts as shortage and scarcity, the intellectual domain of the economist. And yet economists have had rather little to say about corruption, the recent explosion of interest in business ethics excepted. One obvious explanation for this is the disparity between fragmented, anecdotal and qualitative evidence necessarily characteristic of corruption and the mathematical sophistication of much contemporary economics. The neglect of specific consideration of corruption may simply indicate its tacit or its unscrutinised incorporation: 'normal market forces' comprise not only the 'invisible hand' of supply and demand but also the forces of corruption. Economics subsumes the racket into the market rather than thinking about it, as was remarked upon in contemporary discussions of the Nigerian cement racket of the mid 1970s (Anon, 1977, 223).

What economists (and others) have recognised is that there are particular instances of corruption of economic significance. In communist Europe bribes and backhanders from branch managers faced with a scarcity of inputs kept wheels turning which otherwise would have stopped. Corruption is generally seen as playing a part in keeping things going in authoritarian régimes effectively but by no means optimally. This is one element in Leff's description (1964, 11) of corruption as a 'hedge against uncertainty', the decision taker's tool for smoothing out fluctuations generated by other people's decisions. This interpretation runs counter to a broader based assertion that corruption enhances rather than diminishes uncertainty, especially as far as the operationalisation of policy is concerned. Lastly Bhagwati (1974, 49) provides a thoroughly economic interpretation in terms of the superiority of price incentives over legal incentives. The hope has sometimes been expressed in the third world context, and is equally applicable to the post-communist situation, that the rise of business will lead to a diminution of corruption: that hope is weakly supported by the evidence.

A common thread of these accounts is an assumed and necessarily rough and ready cost benefit analysis. Bribes seem to pay, certainly at the individual level, and to anticipate later discussion, some would argue that the same is true for the community at large. In this latter case the immediate rejoinder is to suggest that consideration of what does and what does not contribute to the analysis is somewhat biased. The underlying and very cynical assumption is of the political and administrative order as a market place in which 'every man has his price'. Not only in Walpole's England - described by Acton (1956, 231) as 'a monarchy that throve by corruption' - but in much of the present day world however the assumption is not unrealistic even though it eventually eliminates any meaningful concept of corruption fusing it with that of the market. The question of costs and benefits will however be returned to when arguments as to functionality or dysfunctionality are considered.

The undoubted entrepreneurial element in the practice of corruption has invariably been favoured by circumstances of rapid economic and social change. Thus the great cities of the New World in their periods of most rapid growth, the second half of the nineteenth century for example, were deservedly notorious for high levels of corruption gaining a reputation which successive reformers have not been able wholly to redeem. Government structures were unable or deliberately unwilling to cope with new tasks in such areas as roads and housing and were superseded by corrupt institutions and processes. The situation is remarkably complementary to that in communist Europe, a different political and economic if not social situation but one characterised by rapid urbanisation and by the official system's inability to deliver. Rapid urbanisation is also characteristic of the third world in the post-colonial situation and may even be seen as the apex of its corruption. However for its understanding the pre-independence period of equally fast albeit less conspicuous change in which new élites established themselves, not least by corruption, is equally important. Finally Vietnam in the years since reunification provides another present day example (*FEER*, 25 June 1992 and 11 July 1996). What had been, at least in the North, a relatively corruption free society has become evidently corrupt. This was the case with customs - one pool of officers reaped $20000 a month - and import licensing, access to health and education, building permits and visas. Among proffered explanations are: demise of revolutionary zeal, the involvement of powerful actors, the legal and bureaucratic system and its inability to handle even the partial shift from communist to market economy, low salaries, nepotism (family and party), and limited protection of 'whistle blowers'. In all these circumstances the inadequacies of the economic, political and social structures are overcome by *ad hoc* processes of corruption, processes which normally gain a momentum enabling them to survive the official resolution of the crisis in the guise of reform but at the expense of damaging the reputation abroad of a country whose future growth depends on international investment.

The essence of this interpretation which develops from a very narrow and specific 'poverty' account is then inadequacy of political structure and process, the emergence of entrepreneurial élites who bridge the gaps in such areas as welfare and employment by corrupt methods which gain momentum strong enough to survive, albeit diminished, eventual reforms. This in turn poses the question of durability. Public opinion and concerted political action have made for example Australian and North American cities less corrupt than a century ago, and in the latter instance the word 'reform' at least in the municipal context came to have a specifically anti-corruption connotation. Whether the same will be true of the third world remains to be seen, whether the more extreme corruption (whatever its moral or functional status), authoritarian political structures, and material poverty will inhibit reform processes and destroy the optimistic perspective which sees corruption as an intrinsically transient phenomenon remains to be seen. As yet the evidence is not encouraging.

In a recent book Ting Gong (1994) outlines a position which she calls, perhaps misleadingly, the 'policy outcomes perspective', arguing that at least in China corruption - and the argument is also restricted to bureaucratic corruption - arises from the incompatibility of the régime's general and organisational policies. In other words it is the intended outcome of the pursuit of an economic growth policy by a government organised on traditional communist lines. It is neither structures nor individuals (and their morality) which bring about corruption, but their interaction.

Class

There remain to be considered two important causal accounts of corruption in terms of class and conspiracy. As a starting point for the first of these consider the fact that corruption, except at the petty level, always advantages and is promoted by a small group of practitioners. Some are inside the political apparatus, others are outside but well connected to it under a variety of names, expeditors (Panda, 1978, 62), fixers, agents, *compradors*, *tolkach* (Ward, 1989, 62), middlemen. They are professional (yet irregular) brokers of political and administrative decisions. Price is what differentiates them from lobbyists - the bribe is offered rather than the argument - though the distinction may be less clear in practice than in precept. This group, or class to anticipate the Marxist focus (Anon, 1981, 196), might in the first instance be regarded as consequence or concomitant rather than cause. They become the latter when they become dominant rather than parasitic and when their aims and interests take over from production and process as the very heart and rationale of the political and economic order. Taken this far the argument runs counter to a more conventional view of corruption as part of a plural system, which it undoubtedly is in say France or New Zealand. But in many instances corruption as the heart and mind of the system, 'corruption rather than investment ... the major source of financial gain', looks to be a more perceptive description, in much of the third world for example. Kameir and Kursany (1985) elaborate this in Marxist terms for the Sudan, describing corruption as the fifth factor of production and in class rather than individual terms. An itself unproductive class has seized the lion's share of the surplus - an idea also present in Davidson's writings on Africa (1992, 229) - after international monopoly capital has had its first cut. Corruption is viewed by Kameir and Kursany as 'a means for the distribution of the national income' (1985, 8) necessarily rather than incidentally a bulwark of totalitarian rule as it requires the state 'to undertake costly repressive measures on behalf of the benefiting parasitic class' (1985, 10-11). This view runs counter to that which sees corruption as part of a plurality of system maintaining activities; it is the pre-eminent activity. The authors exemplify their argument with reference to urban development, banking and transport. At its very least their analysis is a shrewd evaluation of extreme cases applicable for example to Zaire, Burma and until recently Mexico. Gould (1980, 7) uses Zaire as a vehicle for a more thoroughly Marxist interpretation of corruption, in which corruption and underdevelopment are dialectically linked components of the same process of reproducing the capitalist mode of production. Others describe the same situation in terms which are theoretically more neutral if often polemic: Lamine (1979, 94) writes of '*une bourgeoisie naissante, composée essentiellement de fonctionaires* (a rising bourgeoisie of officials); Andreski (1966, 62-9) writes of Latin America's 'kleptocracy'; an Indian opposition MP, quoted by Monteiro (1966, 15) of 'a phytogerontocracy without ethical standards or moral values - a corrupt, inefficient, perquisite grabbing top class weighing down on the mass of people'. This position accords with another India based view, of the economist Bhagwati (1974, 63), that corruption favours agency activities over production activities. It can also be related to Weber's argument that the end of the medieval period witnessed a shift from a quest for economic gain via political exploitation or monopoly to a quest rooted in rational activity and small but steady returns (Momsen, 1974, 13).

Such élite explanations are convincing in general terms but they do call for three qualifications. Not all élites are corrupt is the simplest and most obvious of these but requires to be stated. Even corrupt élites are not necessarily motivated solely by self-interest: the political aristocracy of eighteenth century Britain (though not necessarily their continental counterparts) comfortably combined corrupt practice with an undoubted sense of public interest. Thirdly corrupt élites are not constant in their composition but subject to change in both the short and long terms. Competition between rival élites is the essence of both democratic and non-democratic politics.

In these terms political corruption in the third world and more generally turns back the clock several hundred years. When Williams (1987, 4) argues that in Africa at or about the time of independence an élite raised the drawbridge in terms of access to power thereby necessitating the emergence of a fixer group or class he was following the same line. Historically Waquet (1991, 83) notes that in seventeenth and eighteenth century Florence corruption may be viewed as a bourgeois-élite transformation, the emergence of such a class, an interpretation paralleled by Scott (1972, 27-9) for seventeenth century England. Panter-Brick (1978, 172-3) notes its embryonic presence in Lenin's *Imperialism*. Rostovtzeff explains Rome's decline in terms of the diversion of creative energy away from production towards 'shrewd exploitation of a position of privilege within the state' (Rostovtzeff, 1957, Vol. 1, 530). The argument is also not unreasonably applied to the *nomenklatura* of the now vanished communist régimes. Writing of the transition to the market economy in Poland Kochanowicz (1993, 244) writes: 'I do not have in mind the simple bribery of bureaucrats ... but the more general behaviour pattern of peripheral élites who, transforming themselves into a "state bourgeoisie", turn the state into a revenue raising instrument in order to secure the upper middle class standard of living of the advanced societies'. Nor is this a wholly unfair description of the large and expanding body of lobbyists, public relations experts, lawyers, advisers, consultants and quangoists who stalk corridors of power from Washington to Wellington. They are open to the same accusation as to the essence of their role even when scrupulously honest in such matters as bribes. The essence of all these arguments - and I suspect one basis of their popular appeal - is that a small and privileged and self sustaining group - sometimes but by no means invariably the bureaucracy itself - have hi-jacked the political system for their own ends, an explanation which carries conviction while allowing the majority off the hook of responsibility. The most general version of the argument deserves the last word: corruption is 'a levy imposed on the labour of producers by the occupants of the power structure' (Revel, 1987, 36).

Conspiracy

Conspiratorial explanations have so instinctive a popular appeal that they share with much of the anecdotal evidence of corruption the need to be considered with a dash of scepticism and caution. Conversely mention of conspiracy in the scholarly community and in the context of organised crime is too often dismissed as scaremongering. In fact such an account is not merely the creation of sensationalist media. Alatas (1990, 131) quotes the prestigious Kefauver Committee of 1950-51 with approval: 'organised crime goes hand in hand with organised corruption'; and Benson (1978, 236-7) describes organised crime as 'corruption's largest single cause'. The context is specific, organised crime in the USA, but the evidence is overwhelming, the organised corruption of the police in particular and the justice process in general by professional criminals. It is also often asserted that organised crime begins in machine politics. The phenomenon however is not exclusively American; it is familiar enough in Marseilles and Melbourne if less evidently so, or overwhelmed by other issues, in the third world. An Australian authority sees organised crime and official corruption as essentially associated (Dickie, 1988, 265). The word 'organised' here deserves note. What we here discuss is not the corruption of individuals by individuals - the police constable by the pimp for example - the true and infrequent instance of the 'bad apple' - but rather corruption of whole agencies or their directing groups or whole political parties by criminal groups dominant or seeking dominance within say city or province.

Almost always such corruption begins with the cluster of activities known as vice - prostitution, pornography, drugs, illegal gambling - in situations where law and regulation runs counter to at least a substantial or influential segment of popular opinion and practice. Payment of bribes to enable operations to carry on is lucrative to both sides, and as it usually quickly connects with municipal government so corruption in the 'vice' sector is also a launching pad for entry to other sectors, public works (Alexander and Caiden, 1985, 30) and most notoriously the waterfront, in Melbourne and New York for example. Every city of size and substance has a 'vice' industry and its geographical manifestation, a 'red light district', regulated, located and occasionally repressed in terms of potentially corrupt interaction between operators and officials. It also has law enforcement agencies and their political controllers with particular policies and practices, almost invariably incorporating a degree of tolerance - whatever vice's legal status - and usually some corruption. The outcome is of course a particular, and sometimes conspicuous geography. In such terms the organised crime explanation of corruption stands up to scrutiny at several scales: it becomes more controversial as its scope widens.

Firstly police corruption is obviously a peculiarly pernicious phenomenon which readily expands from a base in 'vice' to embrace and undermine the whole enterprise of law enforcement, corruption itself included. A presently much publicised instance is New South Wales. It must however be recognised at this point that the concept of policing is itself one which can be operationalised and interpreted in a great variety of ways. At the very least the question on whose behalf the police operated - in principle and in practice - must be asked at the start of any particular discussion of police corruption. More controversially it has been suggested that by corrupt means powerful yet superficially respectable groups have taken control of government for their own ends without rousing public awareness. This is at least a parallel version of the class argument previously discussed. The usual scholarly reaction of dismissive scorn - 'reds under the beds' for example - is of course to the conspirator's advantage. The phenomenon certainly raises the issue of the limits of the legitimate pursuit of self interest by any group which gains political power, a matter of opinion more than of fact. Yet a more complete acceptance of conspiracy theories appears in the writings of scholars and statesmen who could scarcely be viewed as alarmist or naïve. Moynihan (Benson, 1978, 92) asserts that the United States government is 'at many levels controlled by massive and sinister commercial interests' citing as evidence the reluctance of Dewey, Harriman and Kennedy, whose reputation was made as 'organised crime' busters to sustain such a role in very high office. Chambliss (1978, 6) provides a more detailed account at (Washington) state level: 'organised crime may not be something that exists outside the law and government but may instead be a creation of them'. That might be asserted of many authoritarian régimes even though recognition would needs be given to corruption's role in making the unworkable work. It is less credible to interpret the USA or Italy, an outstanding contemporary example of the eventual collapse of a contemptuous attitude towards conspiracy explanations, in these latter terms. Chambliss (1978) and Benson (1978) explore manipulations of potentially fair, honest and workable systems for the benefit of a privileged few and the disbenefit of the majority, a situation close enough to the class theory and distinct from it, if at all, only in the composition and the covert character of the operators. A conspiratorial interpretation is more convincing and more general and closer to home than our prejudices would wish to allow, uncomfortably evocative of the disturbing, dispiriting and too easily ignored fact that the most successful acts of corruption are the most secret.

Although this discussion of cause contains a number of convergences - of bureaucracy, class and conspiracy for example - yet it certainly forces the abandonment of any reductionism or monocausality. It also necessitates the expansion of simplistic perspectives into wider issues, inequality in this case. The phenomenon of political corruption presupposes the existence of the corruptible individual but recognises his or her explanatory power as limited - and not everyone has a price - unless placed and considered in a particular political structure which may be more or less corruptible. It is the consideration of structure as at least as important as the individual which is the significant step beyond a particular perspective in this case. As to direct causes the mobilisation and exploitation of inequalities expressed in such terms as class, sectional interest and conspiracy characterise and summarise a rich variety of situations as being in essence the capture of the political and administrative apparatus for private gain returning us not only to the moral element but also to our definitions.

The geographer exploring and considering corruption at once feels at home in this multi-causal and multi-connected landscape. Some issues are unfamiliar: few geographers are moral philosophers. Others such as third world poverty, social and economic inequality (and its spatial dimension) and processes of urban growth are part of geography's mainstream. The geographer's particular contribution, exemplified in an earlier chapter, is to recognise that these are the condition of particular places as well as broad generalisations, that Australia is differently corrupt and for different reasons from New Zealand and Canada, Burma from Thailand, Malaysia and China, because though neighbours they differ in environment, resources, history and social order.

Geography is not then a cause of corruption but it does in part account for its spatial variation. It is as different places that the instances mentioned above are differently corrupt and some of them might reasonably be described as corrupt spaces. The causes of corruption do have a geography, of the whole practice of government and of the ways and means of public participation therein within the United States to cite one of the more explored examples, of the experience of European emigrant settlement and resultant urbanisation in the New World, even of half a century of communist bureaucracy which failed to eliminate difference in central Europe. It is this dimension which attracts and invites geographical exploration rather than naïve geographical explanation.

8 The consequences of political corruption

Any account of corruption must eventually proceed from definition, characterisation, description and cause to explore results. It is moreover these results, controversial as they are, which provide the subject with real world importance over and above its purely intellectual significance. In any event the intellectual shapelessness of the subject which derives from its extent, fragmentation and concealed character begins to be resolved when empirical evidence is explored and consequences are examined. This chapter is firstly an examination of major categories of political corruption at scales from the personal to the geopolitical and then of exercises in measurement and scale. The debate as to functionality or otherwise is reserved for the next chapter.

Considerations of scale

At the extremes of the spectrum no great difficulty arises as to the consequences of corruption. At the personal level the very nature of corruption is to increase the means of the few - often a famous few, Marcos and Mobutu for example - at the expense of the many, and of the rich at the expense of the poor. It must however be admitted that in the context of third world petty corruption rich is an inappropriate phrase for the process of modest elevation (to say nothing of the wider depression) of living standards in the struggle to meet family needs and obligations. Where at higher levels enrichment is the right word then the question of destination arises, investment or expenditure, a question which relates importantly to questions of functionality. Some commentators on the third world regard this as in some sense the central issue: to Mèdard 'the real question is the use of the money' (1986, 129). In practice the wages of corruption are used for both consumption and investment, on luxuries and on necessities. In the third world for example land and buildings are the not uncommon investment destination of ill gotten gain destined to meet such obligations as school fees for example and also an insurance against being found out and punished. Ostentatious expenditure and offshore remittance are often more significant destinations even allowing for exaggeration generated by the fact that accounts of fast cars and fast women lose nothing in the telling and for jealousy or even social conscience. It is not necessarily easy however to draw the line between investment and consumption. The luxury *dachas* and cottages of the *nomenklatura* are a real and durable addition to national wealth but would scarcely have ranked high in national investment priorities. For wine, women and song there is no such apologia or ambiguity. Nor is the relationship constant: Hao and Johnston assert that the investment rather than consumption of the proceeds is a new feature in the resurgence of corruption in China (Hao and Johnston, 1995, 137-8). One other regional exception also deserves notice: it has been asserted that there is an evident tendency in Latin America to use the proceeds of corruption to begin in business, true capital formation (Little, 1992, 63).

The Economist, 17 February 1996

Ostentatious expenditure notwithstanding the proceeds of corruption are also a matter for secrecy and concealment. This may take the simplest of forms, bullion or jewellery in a safe deposit. Recent burglaries of safe deposit companies in London have generated a surprisingly small number of claimants, testimony to their dubious role as lodging places for dishonestly (probably sometimes corruptly) acquired wealth. Money may be laundered via race courses and casinos. Most commonly it will be despatched offshore, not only to avoid discovery but also to evade taxation and as insurance against future needs in the event say of a change of government. The very act of transfer may itself be illegal and corrupt but the scale of such transactions, discussed below, appears very large. In most third world countries the phenomenon is essentially post-colonial. As Williams notes prior to independence not only was corruption modest and normally petty but export receipts not remitted to the producer country were held in sterling or franc accounts (Williams, 1987, 47). There was also strict and honest exchange control. The traditional destination of the proceeds of corruption is the numbered Swiss bank account. Now as that destination has attracted criticism and remedial action it is more likely to be one of the micro states or micro-dependencies, the Cayman Islands or Lichtenstein for example, whose secretive banks and trust companies are an important segment of their economies.

The central question in this context returns us to Mèdard's assertion and is in fact unanswerable save in the most general terms. Has this outflow of assets in general, and from our perspective in its corrupt component, played a significant role in the lowly economic status of these countries? What if that sum of money had been available for domestic investment and even more what if it had been wisely invested? The first of these was once an unasked and even taboo question to which the answer is now a qualified but unquantifiable yes. What is the significance of bribes in the context of the inflow of capital in such terms as quantity, location and destination? At the very least these are promising, if in practice difficult, research agendas.

At the other extreme the question may reasonably be asked of the global consequences which are implicit in the preceding discussion even as it focuses on individuals. The evidence is equivocal: Britain and the United States at least began to prosper in circumstances of widespread corruption, and neither has been able fully to rid its political and economic system of the condition while massively reducing its apparent presence. Rome was almost proverbially undermined by corruption and its role in the collapse of European communism is often referred to. More speculatively it has been suggested that Italian military weakness and unpreparedness at the start of World War Two owed something to corruption. Imagine the geopolitical consequences of an effective ally for Hitler in the Mediterranean in 1940-42. Similarly South Vietnam was weakened by the extent of corruption (Alatas, 1990, 135) undermining the effectiveness of American money, manpower and machines. Comparison with the Malayan emergency of the post-war years where and when there was relatively little corruption may be revealing here. At the macro scale Elwert argues that corruption undermines the credit generating capacity - and I would add political credibility - of African countries so it uncouples that continent from world markets (1993, 18). Nor should discussion be confined to the scale of geopolitics. Regional development in post-war Britain was the domain of many corrupt politicians and officials. An informant told me a convincing tale of new textile machinery destined for regional development in Ulster in the 1960s and subsidised as such but which by means of well placed bribes ended up in South African factories competing with British carpet makers. This is not to venture a new corruption based theory of geopolitics or industrial location. It is simply to suggest that corruption has a place at a variety of scales.

Between as well as at these two extremes the geographer's distinctive role is to ask the question 'what is where and why?'. Political corruption is part of the answer, and a neglected part, across a whole range of phenomena, the visible landscape and the less directly observable spatial patterns which are at the heart of geography. In every British or North American city the pattern of suburbs and streets, shops and factories is not quite - sometimes not at all - what planners and politicians intended. If as Bertrand Russell (1938, 5) asserted politics is about intended effects then corruption is an apolitical phenomenon, for corruption generates deviation and uncertainty as well as difference. The same is true of the spatial order in the post-communist world and the third world and will of course continue to be so since the decisions taken on a corrupt basis so often concern durable elements of landscape and society.

Rural

A traditional albeit arbitrary starting point for fuller discussion is the rural sector, an unusual starting point since most discussions of corruption conclude, even after allowing for under-reporting, that corruption is more an urban than a rural phenomenon. From a European or North American perspective they may be right - but recall the popular reputation of farm subsidies - and there is reason to believe that elsewhere the rural dimension is as much underexplored as underestimated. Land reform was central to Mexico's institutionalised revolution and doubtless initially well intentioned but its operation has always been profoundly limited and its practical success constrained, and can only be understood as such, by extensive bribery and corruption. Much the same is true in general terms of rural land and land reform in the third world. The colonial power commonly provided a more or less honest land survey, prepared for revenue purposes, but the grass roots operation of which was often characterised by a petty corruption which has grown rather than diminished. As custodians of vital information and essential skills land registry clerks, surveyors and agronomists have been powerfully placed: their corruption as well as that of politicians and administrators has played a part - but how large a part? - in for example the failure of Mexican and Burmese agriculture in otherwise quite favourable circumstances. The phenomenon is not purely of the present. The settlement of rural land in the New World has a history of corrupt officials and politicians, corrupt settlers and even corrupt if more often corrupted indigenous peoples. And this occurred in a context which in deliberate reaction to the Old World situation emphasised openness and accessibility. A caveat must however be entered as to the parallel impact of incompetence and inexperience. The land registrar in the Canterbury settlement (New Zealand) who chose to site his office in an inaccessible location was eccentric and inept, not, as far as we know, corrupt. But there is no reason to believe that corruption is or was absent in the rural sector more generally. The forces that drove corruption in communist Europe were as present for state farms as for state factories, for peasant farmers as for production line workers. The development of ever more elaborate structures of farm support, subsidy and protection invites fraud of which corruption is surely a part. The Common Agricultural Policy notoriously exemplifies this situation, with fraud currently estimated at 10 per cent of revenue, of which fraud corruption, more exactly defined, is certainly a significant part. Absolute estimates vary hugely: in 1993 an official EU report suggested £198 million but the President of the Court of Auditors put forward £6 billion, a factor of thirty (*FT*, 18 May 1993). In this context fraud (as well of course as the subsidies themselves) has direct geographical impacts, on land-use patterns, tobacco growing in south-eastern Europe for example (*The Observer*, 20 June 1995), as well as reflecting considerable variation in member country's levels of political commitment to an assault on the problem.

Urban

There are more parallels between urban and rural political corruption than might initially be expected, in such areas as complexity - planning ordinances may rival the Common Agricultural Policy in this respect - and continuity. This latter deserves particular note in the planning context since policy changes, especially those which are generated in committee are often misinterpreted as evidence of corruption. Unwise as such procedures may be in opening up a seemingly inexplicable gap between public policy and practice, they are not corrupt. In developed countries and especially in situations and regions of urban growth and change the world of town planning is a domain where corruption is not uncommon and accusations are even more frequent. This is more accurately depicted in the media and the courts than in the literature or even than in discussion with professionals. The fundamental problem has already been mentioned: how can decision takers remain honest when with salaries of tens of thousands of dollars they may be approached by developers, local or international, whose stake (and resources for corruption) can be measured in millions. This is an area where official reaction extends from complacency, in Britain and New Zealand for example, to well articulated concern in North America. One reason why corruption is in general taken very seriously in the USA is that it is publicly perceived and experienced as a deep seated phenomenon never so fully or effectively eliminated from government as it was in Britain. The idea of the importance and potential of corruption is a central theme in Americans' political perceptions. Thus Paul, a Miami lawyer, describes land-use zoning as 'the biggest single corruptor of the nation's local governments' (*New York Times*, 13 May 1975): Gardiner and Lyman sum up the results in geographical and economic terms: 'developments where people don't want them or where communities aren't ready for them ..... it is something we all pay for' (Gardiner and Lyman, 1978, 202). As Amick (1976, 78) observes: 'citizens living in those (corrupt) areas will simply not enjoy the quality of life they would have enjoyed had they been getting a fair share from their public officials'. The comments may be American but their logic is universal. The fact that planning codes and laws are inevitably imperfect, that in a few cases critics and corruptors have logic, as well as in the latter case money, on their side modifies the argument but does not overthrow it. Corruption moreover does not act solely and directly via zoning decisions turned into actual land-use changes. It operates also, and at times more significantly, via changes in land values (Gardiner and Lyman, 1978, 79-80) where advance information is usually the key, and also via standards of construction, a link to the other major area of corruption contracts. The very reputation and tradition of a jurisdiction as corrupt in this respect may be more important and more lasting as an inhibitor of good planning than any particular corrupt actions.

The situation examined above is not peculiar to liberal democracies as planning in the broader sense characterises a diversity of political systems. Thus the social services in communist Europe, housing, health, schools were in principle thoroughly and rationally planned, but in practice corruption was an important element of the allocation process as well as being a contributor to defects in planning. The expansion of third world cities contains a formal as well as a much better known spontaneous component and in both sectors corruption is a major force. The Delhi Development Authority has been called 'the most corrupt institution in the country. A recent crackdown destroyed 10000 unauthorised buildings on 1200 acres (*FEER*, 4 May 1995). Acquisition of land, access to licences in for example provision of public transport, access to infrastructure all have an unofficial price as well as a regular procedure, and the practitioners of the corrupt side, the givers and takers of bribes, have a strong interest in maintaining their investment and restricting the effectiveness of their official counterpart. It is true of course that much of this third world development - and even a part of that in the communist world - metamorphoses over the years from irregularity, corruption and seeming squalor, to a legal and even attractive state, some informal urban growth in Latin America for example. The fact remains that corruption has been an intrinsic part of the process and has left an indelible mark, in the location of facilities for example, and that it was one obstacle to the implementation of more rational procedures which might have had a better outcome and which certainly cannot be dismissed as unrealistic or idealised.

Transport

Not only the production but also the movement of goods and services is a sphere for corruption. An obvious and commonplace contemporary example is bribery of officials charged with exchange control, immigration and customs functions, notably in the third world. The opportunity to profit from such positions places these departments high in the order of preference of many entrants to the public service. The bribery of customs officials in the third world is especially significant since this particular revenue, old established and cheap to collect, is often central to the tax system as well as having close connexions with a variety of illicit activities, drugs and arms for example. But sadly ease of collection equates with ease of corruption. This topic has been most thoroughly looked at by Bhagwati (1974, 62-3) who notes its more profound effects: discouraging the optimal use of existing capital and redistributing profit from production to agency oriented activities as well as simply raising the cost of doing business. At the same time its important surface characteristics should not be discounted, the avoidance of delay, the flouting of inconvenient laws and regulations, and most simply the immediate and particular reduction of costs whatever the broader and longer term implications.

This is one area where the durable impact of decisions made in the past must be recognised. A particularly good example is the construction of railways and tramways - and perhaps now the regulation of successors - in the late nineteenth and early twentieth centuries when promoters and land owners were often conspicuously successful corrupters of decision makers. Cannon (1966, 39-46) writes of late Victorian Melbourne: 'hardly a member of parliament whose vote could be bought went without his bribe in the form of a new railway, a spur line, or advance information on government plans to enable him to buy choice land in advance'. He goes on to suggest that an immediate consequence was an operating loss of £1000 per day in the 1890s. Predictably the USA was similarly corrupt at every level from tramway to transcontinental. Now more is heard of road construction: When Long ran Louisiana roads cost twice as much per mile as in an adjacent state and were of inferior quality (Benson, 1978, 192). When Ghana gained independence the ruling party ran new main roads through towns where its supporters were concentrated (Fitch and Oppenheimer, 1966, 107). In every instance however corruption has generated a difference in the landscape, and in many cases an ongoing cost burden derived from less than optimal spatial location and patterning. An important secondary cost was the time taken to sort out the mess: the corrupt affairs of the never built La Crosse and Milwaukee railroad (under 1856 land grant legislation) involving $105 million took a quarter of a century to resolve (Current, 1976, 244-50).

Environmental

The environmental context of corruption has already been alluded to in several respects, forestry in the third world, the notoriety of the waste disposal industry (Alexander and Caiden, 1985, 90). This latter is an environmentally and politically sensitive operation in which bribery is used at several levels, to facilitate disposal of 'difficult' kinds of refuse, to overload facilities, to gain salvage rights. At the other extreme the teak forest cases exemplify the bribe's role in gaining access to environmentally sensitive but also very lucrative resources in the face of legal protection. A discussion with a Western Samoan evinced a comprehensive catalogue of instances of corruption with environmental impact: privatisation of traditional title to land to enable development, cattle ranching without prior environmental investigation (nepotism in this case), post-cyclone public works of indifferent quality at too high a price. Central Europe under communist rule became notorious for the extent of pollution, the product not only of poor legislation and inadequate technology but of a command economy in which output at any price was pre-eminent and in which managers and officials bribed or were bribed to this end. Switching off pollution control was part of this process. In the democracies where so often high population densities and high levels of economic activity stress the environment to the limit the case for environmental management receives widespread support, but it is not necessarily welcome at a personal level. There is no scarcity of people wishing say to build a house on a vulnerable coast or an area of high scenic value and prepared to bribe to do so. Allegations of this kind are common. Environmental protection requires public acceptance as well as good laws and an effective executive. Corruption is a means of expression available to the powerful of their dissent from such consensus and their preference for their own ends.

Measurement and scale

The 'cost' of corruption is often considered, and the idea of cost-benefit analysis is pivotal (albeit impracticable in exact terms) to evaluation of the role of corruption. Nevertheless estimates in monetary or percentage terms are neither common nor at the heart of most discussion of the topic. This is unsurprising: corruption is a secret and secretive practice which aims to leave no traces. Ideally it proceeds on a word of mouth and cash in hand basis. Everything is against the scholarly enquirer for there are also good reasons to believe that what such evidence exists combines understatement, exaggeration and a long standing preference for round numbers. When an undoubted expert advises a Transparency International gathering that 'the average level of bribery of 5 per cent is heading towards 15 per cent' (Transparency International, 1994, 3) he is not expecting to be taken literally but is able to justify the numbers in general terms. On occasions there is problem within problem: how big is the informal sector and how much of it is corrupt? The growing body of literature on the informal sector does not greatly concern itself with this latter question either in simple quantitative terms or as a question of the extent to which corruption is essential to viability. The task is finally complicated by the poor quality of official statistics, by accident and design, in many countries. Unlike scholars those engaged in corruption have no interest in the truth, even less in the exact truth, and least of all in its getting out. Unsurprisingly some undoubted experts abandon all idea of measurement: 'the loss to the public is colossal and impossible to estimate' (Alatas, 1990, 150).

The initial reaction may then well be to question the worthwhileness of any such exercise, and it has to be admitted that it cannot go very far, provides no basis for the construction of sophisticated models, and rouses rather than satisfies our morbid curiosity. Most literature on corruption says little about exact sums, and fortunately much that is worth saying about the topic can be said in ways not dependent on such an empirical base. That is not to argue that exact information does not matter. Were it available for many third world states the arguments as to the role of corruption in development might be more clearly stated, more nearly resolved. Some of our fundamental distinctions, grand and petty corruption for example, are as much of quantity as of quality. Let us however reiterate the major points: the numbers are always suspect and correlation between what numbers are available and the real significance of the phenomenon is uncertain. But the fascination of the topic is undeniable, at the two extremes of billions of dollars on the one hand and of what can be got for a very modest sum at the other.

To begin with here are three unusually well documented cases: in the Nigerian cement scandal of the mid 1970s the federal government bought cement at a 37.5 per cent premium over market price, and paid demurrage (a fee payable for shipping delays brought about in this case by the sheer volume of the traffic) at a 60 per cent premium often over long periods. This money went to entrepreneurs, agents and civil servants milking the public purse. At one stage about half the ships in the world of the class suitable for long-haul cement traffic were involved in the racket: 360 cement ships waited off Lagos. The typically pyramidal character of such operations is also evident: three major European producers with 78 agents, five Nigerian importers and an unknown but large number of local middlemen handling 81 Defence Ministry contracts. In absolutes the cost was about $1 billion, roughly a quarter of the country's considerable oil revenues at that time (Williams, 1987, 68-71; Anon, 1976, 13-23). Imagine the effect on the country of that sum wisely spent. A British Ministry of Defence case which resulted in the imprisonment of a senior official (Gorden Foxley) in May 1994 involved: at least £1.5 million in bribes; loss of 300 jobs; losses on the sale value of a Royal Ordnance Factory; losses on redundant machinery and lost skills; high prices for a rival product some of which turned out to be unusable; and the costs of investigation (*The Times*, 26/27 May 1994). Estimating a multiplier for the £1.5 million is evidently at best speculative. At the other extreme Lesnik and Blanc (1990, 84-5) tell us what it cost in bribes each month (just one dimension of corruption) to keep an illegal (but productive) factory open in the USSR during the 1980s: 25 roubles each (about $1) to the local militiamen, 500 ($17) to the chief of OBKHSS, 1000 ($35) to the chief militiaman (also covering the public prosecutor), 30 to 50 ($1 to $2 each) to the fire brigade, 100 to 200 ($3 to $7) to the Committee of Popular Control, in total about 1700 roubles a month.

At the upper end of the scale estimates in billions are not uncommon. Thus Cockcroft (1990, 180) connects the build up of $20 billion in African citizens' overseas assets between 1974 and 1985, a period of escalating public debt, with expanding corruption. More recently Ayittey (1990, 235) alleges that $15 billion flees Africa for overseas banks each year, a larger sum than annual foreign aid; and (1990, 235) that Kenyans' overseas assets at $5 billion exceed the country's overseas debt by $1 billion. Eigen quotes $20 billion for African leaders' deposits in Swiss banks in the early 1990s, but goes on to comment that the overall and ongoing cost of bad decisions arising from corruption is probably considerably larger (1993, 9). It has been noted (Heidenheimer, 1989, 786) that for the period 1952-61 there was a rough equivalence between the fortunes made by Latin American presidents and the inflow of aid. In Nigeria in 1992 an estimated $3 billion vanished from the public accounts, a large part of it to corruption, an estimated 10 per cent of Gross Domestic Product (*Economist*, 5 March 1994). Clearly corruption has a macro-economic and thus macro-geographic significance. At the level of the individual enterprise Williams (1987, 99) cites £10 million in the 1980s for a relatively small Nigerian rice company.

Even if substantially overstated and not wholly attributable to corruption the sums are enormous. They are not always consistent: official estimates of CAP fraud are about £200 million a year, unofficially thirty times greater (*FT*, 18 May 1993). For comparison the level in the USA in the restricted area of land-use and building regulation in the mid 1970s was estimated at between $3 billion and $5 billion annually (Gardiner and Lyman, 1978, 11), a large sum but only about $20 per person. Finally two astounding Mexican examples: in 1993 the ruling PRI sought gifts of $25 million each from 29 wealthy men (total $725 million) (Latin American Regional Reports, Mexico and Central America, 22 April 1993) and the country's oil worker unions (and bosses) allegedly gained about $750 million each year from control of access to well paid jobs (Story, 1986, 88). (Trade union corruption it should be added is one of the least studied of all aspects, Australia perhaps excepted.) And yet it has also been observed, notably in Britain, that in terms of outcomes the sums actually paid have often been surprisingly small (Mosley, 1984, 339-41). Doig reports an almost trivial £400 an acre for planning permission to build in north east England c. 1980, less than £100 per building plot (Doig, 1984, 185-7).

Turning to percentages the commonest assertion is that at every level government may be exposed to 'cuts' of a few per cent in such areas as licensing, purchases and contracts, the proceeds divided between legislators, civil servants, suppliers and sometimes political parties. The *Financial Times* on 5 May 1993 suggested a rule of thumb 5 per cent for access to important people in the third world, 5 per cent of $200000 to a senior official, of $200 million to a prime minister. Actual instances vary enormously: the formal sector in Peru pays 1 per cent, but the informal 10-15 per cent (de Soto, 1989, 154-5); 2 per cent of salary to the party by political appointees in Indiana in the 1970s (Amick, 1976, 124); 4 per cent on Ghanaian import licences in the same decade; and 4 per cent on public works contracts in New South Wales in 1991 (Maiden, 1991, 261-2); 17.5 per cent on North Sea oil contracts (Andvig, 1995, 310-11). Most instances of higher levels are third world: 20 per cent to 100 per cent over the market price is Klitgaard's assertion (1988, 39); forty times their salary received in bribes by the most favourably placed irrigation engineers in southern India and one to five times as the norm according to Wade (1984, 14-15). Aid is widely regarded as particularly corruption prone: 'in an average development project it is not rare to observe that only 30 per cent of the total grant is actually spent on the project' (Mèdard, 1986, 128). Elwert (1993, 16) quotes a Zairean example, the Inga power station, where the figure was as low as 12.5 per cent. Sadly the same appears to be true of most UN peacekeeping operations. Finally there is some evidence that either the cut is increasing: in Brazil for example where 10 per cent was the norm there is evidence of an increase to 30-40 per cent in the last decade or traditional estimates were too low (Geddes and Neto, 1992, 642). A discussion of the modest resurgence of corruption in Hong Kong in 1992 cites figures of 20 per cent for the police, 25 per cent for government, 55 per cent for private sector (*FEER*, 25 February 1993).

There is no limit to the diversity of quantitative estimates. In Bihar (India) a 1992 (*FEER*, 5 March 1992) estimate suggests that corruption had absorbed half the money set aside for development works since independence and thus gave it a key role in the province's low socio-economic status even by Indian standards. Doig in 1984 (306) found that in Kirby (Liverpool) where illegalities on municipal housing contracts ran to millions of pounds fewer than 1 in 10 of the properties were habitable. This of course extends analysis beyond immediate costs to the immeasurables of human misery, ill health and discomfort and thus to breaking point. Benson (1978, 240) using yet another approach believed that in the mid 1970s between 25 million and 80 million Americans lived in areas where some institutions of local government were fairly continuously corrupt: this might elevate our earlier per person estimate to about $100. Braithwaite estimated in the 1980s that 19 out of 96 (i.e. about one fifth) of Australian government (federal, state and local) regulatory agencies were corrupt. In Britain between 1974 and 1985 five large and thirty smaller local government bodies were involved in litigation relating to corruption (Gillard and Tomkinson, 1980, viii). In this same period one scholar estimates that 75 per cent of Thai parliamentarians were corrupt (Neher, 1977, 484). Finally Barlow (1993, 333-4) attempts to map the network of corruption in a particular eastern seaboard county in the USA in the 1960s and identifies an inner core of six politicians and four officials, with no evident kingpin, extending outwards to involve at least 63 associates and certainly more, at least 32 companies, and as far as New York.

The first hard evidence on the savings to be made by an effective crackdown on corruption has appeared in the 30 August 1996 issue of the *TI National Chapter Bulletin* in the Italian context. The cost of public works contracts has been more than halved, releasing funds for use in other areas. At a more detailed level the San Siro football stadium which was losing 1.5 billion lira annually now returns a profit of 11 billion. Even more spectacular is the report that Uganda's government, following a relatively successful anti corruption drive, was able to collect almost six times as large a tax revenue (more than half from import duties) in 1995 as in 1990 (*Economist*, 27 July 1996). There seems to be no end to the ways of estimating corruption, and estimate is surely a better word than measure; so it must be reiterated that quantitative exemplification is far from being the essence of either the scholarly literature or media accounts. The conclusion to be drawn is superficially banal, that corruption is practically ubiquitous. More profoundly the extent and character of the estimates supports the view that the phenomenon exists and is to be taken seriously as an economic, political, social and geographical force. Even if exaggerated the evidence supports that conclusion as against the traditional albeit now rarely articulated dismissal. Overall the figures support the typically western gut reaction that corruption is a bad thing: developing countries cannot conceivably afford private gain on that scale and in such circumstances; there is no defending a public housing system which delivers at only the 10 per cent level. What however is missing from the debate is estimates from the other side of the equation, of gains and benefits required for the cost-benefit analysis of the functionality or otherwise of corruption to which we now turn.

9 The functions of political corruption

When scholars use such terms as pathological or dysfunctional to describe and evaluate the role of political corruption they make an implicit comparison, of disease as opposed to health, of what works satisfactorily with what works poorly or not at all. The broad mainstream scholarly view of political corruption is an unfavourable one, even to the point of condemnation and indignation. It is a perspective shared by most communities and individuals - at least the principle of honesty is favoured in most cultures - even though the existence of corruption depends on individuals who practise a different code and for whom acts of corruption are clearly functional. As has already been noted the very word corruption has connotations of rottenness and decay which while they may characterise many political systems or institutions would rarely be interpreted as necessary, vital or useful components. There is however an alternative position which begins with consideration of the natural world. Here whatever the associations of the word corruption, decay is a natural, useful, essential and permanent process in the absence of which life would cease. Is the same true, in whole or in part, of the political order? The broad mainstream of scholarship focused upon political corruption would answer in the negative, but the dissenting tributaries present an alternative case which while it is now less cogent and convincing than it seemed to be in its heyday 20 years ago remains worthy of exploration, and which certainly is of fundamental significance.

Essential-permanent-inevitable

Initially however the questions of the essential and permanent roles of corruption are relatively easily disposed of. At least in the broad sense political corruption is not essential: many societies function very well in, as far as can be seen, conditions of its near absence or insignificance. It must be conceded however in anticipation of later arguments, that in some political circumstances corruption appears at the time the only way to get certain things done - recall 'honest graft' -

some of which would on any view be regarded as desirable. As to permanence this may well be the case as far as potential is concerned - the threat of corruption will always be there. But there is ample evidence of the deliberate (perhaps even the accidental) elimination or diminution of corruption - nineteenth century Britain is probably the best and the most fully explored - as well as of movement in the opposite direction. Compare for example contemporary China with China in the early years of communist rule.

The challenge to the conventional wisdom has rather focused upon the usefulness and possibly the inevitability of political corruption at certain stages of development and in certain contexts, asserting that it serves a desirable and otherwise unattainable purpose. The best known examples, Huntington (1968, 59-72) for example, assert that in such contexts as the North American city, especially the city of a century ago, political corruption delivered to the mass of the population a range of services, in summary a system of social and personal welfare, that the official political system could not. Merton (1947, 71-81) saw in corruption an alternative system, alternative to one which was failing to deliver, in which welfare was traded for votes, business and underworld protection for cash, political and career advancement for obedience. As Eisenstadt (1978, 219) succinctly summarises this position, its basis resides in 'the differential between existing political forces and newer social needs'. The focus of this approach is not upon individuals, as victims or as operators, but upon the system, a system whereby, and not only in such well known cases as New York or Chicago for example but also in Denver and Seattle (Benson, 1978, 33), jobs, housing, health care, and for a few movement up the economic and political greasy pole, were offered in return for cash, services and votes, especially by political parties and their leading figures, to often bewildered immigrants. The official political system was feeble by comparison. In this context Jones Ford (1904, 682) reviewing a classic of muck-raking journalism (J.L. Steffens, *The Shame of the Cities*, 1904) provides a typical early functionalist defence: 'the growth of an extra-legal system of connecting the disconnected functions of government for administrative purposes certainly entails corruption, but it does not follow that under such circumstances it is disadvantageous though founded upon venality. Our ordinary system of municipal government is so opposed to all sound principles of business organisation that it is highly creditable to our practical capacity for government that we are able to work it at all. The graft system is bad, but it is better than the constitutional system as established by law'. Note at once that the justification and defence invokes comparison.

The corrupt system served not only to acculturate and assimilate the individual into the American, or Australian, way of life, but also it accompanied and even allegedly underpinned a high rate of economic growth. An analogy with the feudal world from which so many immigrants had come suggests itself, the immigrant becomes again what he had been, to use the medieval phrase, 'that man's man'. He yielded service in return for benefits which were essentially protective. (This of course also suggests that such situations may be interpreted as protection rackets.) The analogy may be sustained through the collapse of 'machine' driven corruption and its supersession by big business and organised crime as comparable to the move from feudalism to capitalism. As Caro (1974, 743-8) argues the older form probably had a closer sense of 'the pulse of block and ward', a better understanding of the finer points of urban geography. This relatively (never totally) benevolent view of corruption argues then that in particular contexts, of place as well as of time, contexts of rapid and often individually bewildering growth and change political corruption functions as a way of delivering essential services which the legitimate system cannot or will not provide.

Evidently the view of political corruption briefly outlined above, and the defence of its functionality, is not peculiar to the nineteenth century New World city. It can be transferred both to the third world and to the communist and post-communist experience. In both instances corruption is often, but by no means invariably, encountered in a context of rapid social and economic change comparable to that discussed above. China is a conspicuous contemporary case, exemplifying the rather inevitabilist view that corruption is no more than a function of a transition which is 'all about reaping private benefit from public assets' (*FEER*, 25 May 1995). Other commentators note that corruption in contemporary China although less than ideal appears better than real world alternatives, but makes no mention of the balance of costs and benefits (Hao and Johnston, 1995). Most pessimistically and again in the Chinese context, but perhaps also more generally in the third world, Cheung (1996, 4-5) argues that corruption is a stage intermediate and transitional between hierarchy rights and property rights, a stage which when it is rooted in regulations and controls (as in India and perhaps more generally in the post-colonial situation) only too easily becomes seemingly permanent. Much of the west by comparison moved cleanly and quickly from the one situation to the other. Cheung's argument falters however when placed in a broader historical context - was the break clean and quick in Europe? - but does not lose all its power with respect to the third world and the question why corruption has not turned out to be a transitory phenomenon. Braguinsky (1996) extends the argument along lines which explain and contrast the transience of corruption in a capitalist environment with its apparent permanence in totalitarian régimes. More generally the existence of elements of functionality in these contexts can scarcely be denied even in the context of overall condemnation. Corruption does provide *ad hoc* solutions to the defects, intrinsic and contrived, of the real world political and economic system as far as the individual is concerned, and when those defects threaten personal survival it is hard to condemn the particular act of individual corruption as dysfunctional or immoral. There is a sense in which corruption keeps things going, and in which movement is better than standstill. This defence is obviously applicable primarily to petty corruption, to the regular low level and low key interaction between citizens and civil servants. Any favourable evaluation of the grand corruption now so commonplace in the third world is much harder to even find let alone defend. (Scott (1972, 90-1) allowed Thailand as a sole exception.) The same is probably true of the communist world in most respects but there too grand corruption may in some cases have played a significant part, as has already been observed, in keeping an economy which might otherwise have stalled in admittedly imperfect motion. Acton's remark that 'official corruption which would ruin a commonwealth serves in Russia as a salutary relief from the pressures of absolutism' (Acton, 1956, 55) adds an historical dimension to the communist experience echoed by Holmes' observation of its safety valve role (1989, 204). It too can equally be applied to much of the third world. The difference between the two systems in this context is that communism formally recognised and tolerated no political alternative and operated with relatively little official flexibility: corruption was usually the only alternative and sometimes a not entirely ineffective one. In the third world there are at least in principle formal and informal political alternatives which have not infrequently been applied. Corruption emerges not as the sole alternative or modification to a non-viable system, but as either component or complement (or in some few cases as the driving force) of a variety of usually personalised and autocratic régimes.

The question of alternatives thus becomes central to consideration of the functionality - and morality - of political corruption, and it is on this basis that to this author at least the functionalist apologia is most convincing in some areas of the communist world, and to some degree at the petty level in the third world. The role of corruption in the demise of communist rule in Europe by comparison with its role as a bastion of the *status quo* in most of the third world also deserves reiteration at this point. In the New World urban context there is much of interest in the view that corruption performed a transient function but it should be pointed out that it was the particular form rather than the essential phenomenon which proved transient. In many of these cities a variety of forms of corruption, but not those of a century ago, continue to thrive. There is almost no evidence that corruption is a transient phenomenon at the individual level. It does not stop simply because needs are satisfied: rather, at the higher levels, it behaves as Parkinson would predict with needs expanding to meet opportunities rather than opportunities being matched to a finite range of needs. The same is true of the third world. Goodman, working in Yucatan in the early 1970s, noted unfavourably the tacit assumption of transience in the functionalist defence (1974, 145-6), an assumption not borne out by subsequent experience, in Mexico and more generally.

Finally it should be observed that views of morality and functionality are necessarily linked with theories of the state. A view of the state as essentially benevolent must result in a hostile evaluation of political corruption. Conversely if the state is viewed as an institution and apparatus of oppression and/or incompetence then corruption as making life more tolerable or corruption as undermining the state, if that be the case and whether by accident or design, may legitimately be defended in its functionalal role. That corruption which maintains the imperfect *status quo* - more often the case in the third world - will reasonably be seen as basically dysfunctional whatever its particular purpose and immediate justification.

Klitgaard (1988, 30-6), a generally unsympathetic commentator with hands on third world experience provides the best summary of the convincing component of the functionalist case. Three useful roles are noted: as a market oriented substitute - there are cases where ability to pay is a more economically efficient approach than application of rules written or unwritten; as a means of minority integration in a hostile (usually urban) context, historically in the growing New World cities but also in other contexts, e.g. Chinese entry into the buoyant capitalism of contemporary Thailand; and as enabling managerial flexibility - the communist world defence. In essence these reduce to particular instances in political circumstances of rigidity or incompetence. To this I would add the occasional role of acts of corruption in the fight to overthrow oppressive and dictatorial régimes.

It is then possible to put a favourable interpretation on political corruption in particular contexts - the gaining of useful ends in difficult circumstances - and in the opinion of some scholars on many occasions and of almost all scholars on a few. Why then has the scholarly consensus, having wavered, returned to a generally hostile assessment of the role of political corruption? Consider in the first instance one of several areas where corruption is conspicuously present and the assessment of its role rarely favourable, bribery within land-use planning. Here corruption seeks to get a different end from that produced by the official system. That system does not need to be perfect to represent a more widely acceptable and socially just result, largely through political channels, than corruption will achieve. As Lowenstein observes government does not need to be perfect to be better than 'the wishes of the highest bidder' (in Heidenheimer, 1989, 34-5). Corruption here replaces the concept of an often well researched public interest with the much narrower one of private gain: it is an alternative to the official system. A central weakness of functionalist defences of corruption is their almost invariable failure to explore available alternatives (and to compare costs and benefits). And such alternatives do usually exist, even if only on paper, and score over corruption on such criteria as rationality, justice and even cost. The difficulty with the alternatives, or counterfactuals to refer back to methodological issues, is that in practice they are so often hypothetical. What if in the heyday of municipal corruption New York or Melbourne had been in the hands of honest men? What would be the social and economic geography of Nigeria in the mid 1990s had so much oil wealth not been siphoned off (and away) by corruption during preceding decades? The criticism of the functionalist defence of corruption that it fails to explore alternatives is an operationally difficult but intellectually cogent one, even though it has to be recalled that the real world is often one where the alternatives cannot readily be implemented or in some cases even discussed.

A second more particular defence relates to capital formation, the business ladder and the trickle down effects of corruptly acquired wealth, a defence of grand rather than petty corruption. It is at once open to criticism in terms of leakage: there is invariably loss in terms of ostentatious consumption and offshore remittance. But a leaky boat may be better than none at all. It is in practical terms a better insurance for the successfully corrupt on a large or medium scale in almost every country to turn that gain into offshore or portable assets against either a change of political fortune or successful legal action than to invest it locally. Latin America has been argued as an exception to this generalisation, despite a tradition of political instability, and ambition to acquire capital has even been proposed as a motivation for corruption. Again the alternatives need exploring: corruption is certainly not the only way and almost certainly an extremely inefficient way of generating capital.

Costs versus benefits

When these arguments have been rehearsed we remain on the edge of the issue even if important ideas such as alternatives have been introduced. Firstly most countries where and while political corruption now flourishes have not prospered. In an extensive statistical exercise Mauro (1995) has demonstrated that corruption lowers investment. Thus, and for other reasons, such countries remain poor or get poorer and corruption even though a prophylactic at the personal level provides no long term solution to their problems. Corruption delivers only in a very limited sense. There are examples - alternatives - which represent a better way which functionalists tend to ignore (Price, 1975, 145). It is surely no coincidence that Singapore and Botswana are both rich and reasonably honest. A second more effective general criticism of the functionalist defence is its limited and fragmentary character (Alatas, 1990, 4) not only in respect of alternatives but also of examination of costs as well as benefits, notoriously difficult though this is in such contexts, of wider consequences as well as particular results, of long term effects as well as immediate issues. Thus Merriam (Benson, 1978, 211-2) noted: 'the boss (openly) gives $100 to charity but (secretly) accepts $1000 for voting against an ordinance for better housing'. Kaminski suggests that though formal cost-benefit analysis is impossible surrogate measures do exist, citing raised mortality indicators in late communist Europe when corruption was at peak levels (1988, 43). Corruption was of course not the only contributor but this particular indicator scarcely suggests a functioning system. The functional defence of corruption invariably highlights the benefits and minimises the costs, emphasises what is functional over what to another group, time or place is not. Its critics provide examples from a variety of contexts: Mèdard (1986, 127) writes of third world countries where 'a hospital is not primarily for treatment or a school for teaching' - the dubious benefit to a few individuals must be set against the cost of an uneducated unhealthy population. Gillard and Tomkinson observe 'corruption means that people live in badly designed inferior housing' (1980, xi); or in more narrowly financial terms 'the city did not get what it paid for ... it certainly paid for what it got' (Caro, 1974, 328). 'Corruption is not a victimless crime' (*FEER*, 11 July 1996). In general terms resources are misdirected towards whatever activities offer the best corruption opportunities. Any kind of cost-benefit analysis at above the individual level, difficult though it is to carry out in precise terms, containing as it must such elements as increased political cynicism and instability (Klitgaard, 1988, 46), comes down emphatically against the functional view if not against every part, individual or occasion. This view that corruption 'is a luxury that developing countries cannot afford' can be traced back to at least 1966, and is one of the basic positions of Transparency International. Goodman particularises this position in terms of inhibition of change and of planning, protection of the inefficient, the fostering of cynicism, the discouragement of critical evaluation of the system, and the rewarding of the knowledgeable (1974, 147-8).

The depravity of corruption

Most magisterially Noonan (1984, 685-706) goes to the heart of the arguments employed in the functionalist defence. He provides an essentially moral denunciation of corruption, ranking it second only to tyranny as the great disease of government. He explores the questionable assumptions of many apologists: does everyone do it? are the needs that are being met the real and important needs? are the consequences as trivial as is sometimes suggested? The culmination of his case is the point that if the arguments employed by the functionalists are sound then no moral ideal can survive. A number of authors echo and expand upon Noonan's position. Caiden (1988, 21) comments upon the internal inconsistencies of most functionalist defences. Key notes that corruption is essentially selfish (in Heidenheimer, 1989, 47). Alexander and Caiden (1985, 154) ask what is its image of the good society? Klitgaard (1988, 210) notes the association of corruption with the abuse of human rights and with racism: 'something is *wrong* in societies where corruption takes over'. Ward, a convert to a hostile view, notes that 'corruption may offer opportunities to the disadvantaged, but sustains underlying unfair structures' (1989, 1). (Bok (1978, 80-1) is similarly scathing as to functionalist defences of lying.) On a rather different philosophical tack Mèdard (1986, 128-9) points out that the functionalist case is often circular: corrupt actions engendered by a corrupt system are needed to make that corrupt system operate. Carino (1986, 192-4) summarises many of these critiques on the basis of work in seven Asian countries:

> ... is corruption tonic in its consequences? On the whole, the answer is negative. Corruption has largely toxic consequences to the organization and the society. We must moderate that statement at the level of the individual who enjoys the extra income of corruption that also gives him an avenue for social mobility as well as more power over the clients and the general

public. Such effects are however positive only in the completely amoral view when greed is allowed to reign supreme ... Corruption clearly entails increased administrative costs through overpayment of supplies and materials and losses in government revenue ... Corruption makes administration difficult as it creates a second line of authority parallel to the formal one, in the process undermining and weakening it. It also results in goal displacement, replacing it with the personal economic interests of the individual employees or the syndicate ... In the society, the first set of harmful effects concerns the losses in the government treasury on both the revenue and expenditure side. ... A second set of harmful effects sets in when corruption renders inutile the intent of policy and regulations. Corrupt civil servants may change target beneficiaries, impose unauthorized controls or fees, or otherwise alter the allocation of values set by law ... The possibility that corruption may improve the economy also seems unlikely since it does not really allow only efficient producers to enter the market ... Our conclusion then is: corruption is toxic, with very few exceptions. We wish we had more positive findings since we are faced with the problem of its strength and pervasiveness in most of the countries we studied ... Perhaps other more sensitive and finer minds can rationalize the existence of corruption. We cannot.

Finally Transparency International, the cutting edge of present day discussion of and action against corruption, argues against the functionalist case in terms of: the exclusion of those unable to pay; its anti-competitive character; its low view of the public service; its degradation of its practitioners; its creation of vested interests opposed to reform. It works only in individual cases and for particular individuals, and 'functions' only within that limited matrix.

Given the weight and diversity of these arguments it is unsurprising that the functionalist position is much less often espoused and articulated now than in the 1970s. 'When we get down to cases we find less disagreement than the academic debate would indicate ... They are for the most part bad' (Klitgaard, 1988, 194). This must also owe something to the events of two decades, a wider awareness of the extent, character and role of corruption in a variety of political contexts during that period and in its association with poverty and repressive political institutions. The diminution of its appeal also relates to the empirical evidence in general, more honest countries are generally faring better and there is almost no present day evidence suggestive of a necessarily and usefully transient role. The philosophical implications of accepting the usefulness and legitimacy of political corruption are frighteningly obvious when articulated. And, to me most convincingly, even the rough cost-benefit analysis which is the only one possible and which is so conspicuously avoided by apologists, comes down heavily against corruption. The fragmentary case for taking a functionalist view of political corruption is just that. In particular instances and places corruption may temporarily act benevolently - though never is it an intrinsically benevolent act - both in the direct and indirect senses. Thus in communist Europe in the 1980s it eased the pains of scarcity and contributed to system change, the case and context where the functionalist view is most readily sustained. More often it serves not to soften or soften up a failing system but as its support and sustenance. The generally conservative character of corruption has already been commented upon. In the domain of political, economic and social governance and development there almost always is another and better way, and corruption stands as an obstacle in its way rather than as a means of its implementation.

10 Cures and controls

If corruption is to be controlled, or even so substantially got rid of that the word cure might be used, then it must first of all be understood. As Sarassoro observes (1980, 10) understanding the causes is the essential preliminary to both prevention and remedial action. Thus if with Benson (1978) we see political corruption as a very serious threat to democracy and rooted in organised crime, then we have at once decided on the scale and direction of any serious measures of investigation and control, not least because organised crime is notoriously reform resistant. Conversely the fitful and poorly focused anti-corruption campaigns of post-war Britain derive from a primarily 'bad apple' understanding of corruption and this explains their limited success. When Mao Tse Tung was in power in China corruption was viewed as having its roots in the individual rather than in the political and social structure and anti-corruption campaigns were thus focused (Hao and Johnston, 1995, 133). Whatever policy and practice be adopted acts of political and administrative will are required which cannot be taken for granted. Where corruption is a serious problem then its perpetrators and their allies will have friends in high places able, overtly and covertly, to obstruct enquiry and remedy. Thus the report of the Santharam Committee, a pioneering, cogent and original analysis and proposal was largely emasculated by India's politicians and senior civil servants evidently anxious to restrict its activities and recommendations to the lower levels of the state apparatus (Dwivedy and Bhargava, 1967, 31 seq; Monteiro, 1966, 71-95). Thailand's Counter Corruption Commission is subject to Prime Ministerial and Cabinet veto (*FEER*, 14 May 1992). There will also be the perennial problems of lethargy, incompetence and complacency. In fairness it must be admitted that an overzealous or misguided campaign against corruption carries important risks such as the witch hunt directed against individuals and/or the stifling of enterprise and initiative (Lethbridge, 1985, 178). A campaign which disrupts the process of government and local administration as occurred in Newark (NJ) in the late 1960s and early 1970s (Amick, 1978, 231) is as destructive as the problem it seeks to remedy.

The problem is as much one for the governed as for the government. The community at large may well prefer a familiar and superficially functional - if occasionally uncomfortable - system of corruption, especially at a modest and petty level, to the unfamiliar and uncertain path of reform. At the other extreme popular pressures or support for control may be primarily punitive or vindictive - 'heads must roll' with greater delight in the rolling than genuine concern for reformation. 'It', whatever it may be, must be taken out of politics (Rogow and Lasswell, 1963, 22) with little thought as to what this means and how this might be done. Nevertheless there is evidence that public tolerance of corruption is diminishing (*FEER*, 23 March 1995 (Editorial)). Finally it should be noted that the benefits of control do not always reside where they might be expected to: those who supply and service oil exploration companies would gain most if corruption, estimated at $35 million annually, were eliminated from the North Sea oil industry (Andvig, 1995, 305).

As a starting point consider a number of lists of cures, remedies or controls. Brabainti (1962, 358-64) suggests: a common morality (as between government and governed); detachment of administration from political pressures; a real knowledge of the job on the part of supervisors; reasonably long tenure of senior posts (or else the chief clerk becomes too powerful!); diffusion of information; legislative oversight; efficient workflow; pride in work; 'an ideology of austerity' (at the personal level); anti-corruption control bodies; and adequate salaries. A near contemporary McMullen (1961) is shorter and more tentative: exemplary action at the top; slightly more police pressure; education; an emphasis on public service; and anti corruption audits. Wraith and Simpkins (1963) in the development context offer a list which is at once more radical and more optimistic: time; education; public opinion; growth of commerce and industry; professionalism; diffusion of wealth and power; central civil service control and inspection; the role and status of the accountant (two decades later strong audit procedures are cited as one of the reasons why Botswana is relatively free of corruption (Charlton, 1990)); law enforcement; and personal integrity and witness. In 1978 Gardiner and Lyman (184), in the specific context of land-use and building regulation in the USA propose: simple policies, visible implementation; good record keeping; disclosure of interest; team work in decision taking; and review of decisions. Quah (1995, 408) suggests six key components of relatively successful campaigns in Hong Kong and Singapore: political commitment, comprehensive measures, an incorruptible control agency, its separation from the police, reduction of opportunity and a well paid civil service. Finally Fitzgerald, a leading Australian investigator of the 1980s, suggests as a minimum: 'ethical leadership, an informed community, a generally open and honest society and efficient methods of detection followed by hard punishment' (Dickie, 1988, 244). The thrust is always towards the reduction of opportunity. A recent formal articulation is Tanzania's *National Integrity Action Plan* (1995) (Langan and Cooksey, 1995, 34-7). Finally mention should be made of Klitgaard's intriguing hypothetical example, developed for teaching at Harvard (Klitgaard, 1984).

A new political morality

Many of these suggestions are pre-eminently practical and/or procedural, efficient workflow carefully analysed by a roving inspectorate, the accountant's role, blacklisting of firms known to have bribed, for example. There is even scope for the Machiavellian: Charlton (1990) reports an instance from Botswana where a corrupt official was not dismissed but forced to stay at his post on terms which forced him to implicate his collaborators. However the main thrust of these lists and of most others is in the direction of changes in basic attitudes and outlook, while yet recalling that corruption control is never more than a secondary governmental and administrative objective (Anechiarico and Jacobs, 1995, 375). There is almost universal agreement that without this, underpinned by a willingness to implement change, in practice nothing can be done. This new political morality is not to be confused with a moralistic approach which tends to focus on individual behaviour, as too does its opposite which sees some forms of corruption as curable by simple decriminalisation (of drugs and pornography for example). 'Appeals to morality' comments Engels (1993, 16) 'are bound to stay ineffective because they presuppose something whose lack is what makes corruption is possible'. The emphasis is rather upon the community, its leaders and its common values, and thus upon public opinion. Thus Sarassoro (1980, 38) remarks that Africa's cure must begin with the state of African society; van Klaveren (Smith, 1964, 197-8) observes (of West Africa) that 'it is not "technical western values" that are needed but civic consciousness and social ethics'; Alatas (1990, 59-60) writes (of Asia) that the problem is not 'insufficient good laws against corruption but that there are insufficient good and powerful leaders to implement them'. Little (1992, 64) regretfully finds evidence of the mobilisation of public opinion against corruption in only three Latin American countries. These examples must not be taken as indicative of a view that this is an exclusively third world problem. The case has been argued that even when corruption was most fully developed in eighteenth century Britain the chief participants never wholly lost a sense of the public good (Heidenheimer, 1989, 62) which sense does seem evidently absent in some third world countries and perhaps too in former communist states (Reed, 1995, 329-30). But more generally the essentials of the above argument are universal rather than particular.

An important consequence of this position is that corruption control must be seen as home grown. That is not to argue that Transparency International, the international business community and aid agencies should cease to think and act in this area: their growing unwillingness to ignore the issue of corruption is to be commended. Likewise there are lessons to be learned, and perhaps now a greater willingness to learn them, from the colonial experience of modest success in corruption control. Simply it is to argue that political and administrative honesty cannot be imposed from outside even though the outside world can provide example and expertise.

What then is required for effective corruption control is leadership exemplary in its integrity, in its sense of public duty and responsibility, and in its political skill; administrative competence; and a community at large which shares and benefits from such a sense of honesty, duty and responsibility and is adequately informed as to the political process of which it is part. The community role may well take the form of the formal mobilisation and organisation of civil society, evident for example in Tanzania's FACEIT (Front Against Corrupt Elements in Tanzania) (Langan and Cooksey, 1995, 105-9). This argument extends beyond the moral to the material, accepting the dimensions already discussed but also asserting their ineffectiveness if the ordinary citizen believes he or she has 'no place in the sun and share in the resources of his country' (Arlin, 1976, 67). The citizen must believe he or she has a stake in the enterprise. As Friedrich observes (1972, 129) 'the degree of corruption varies inversely to consensuality of power' noting also however that the consensuality is often misjudged. If all this tends to an impossible elevation of the role of education, moral, intellectual and practical, it may be pointed out that all the world's great religions propose a programme not basically at odds with these objectives.

An existing political context

These ideas all presuppose both a political pluralism and a rule of law, evidently absent in authoritarian and totalitarian régimes where, by definition, the existing monolithic and arbitrary system is beyond either reproach or debate, not least because it pays its élites so well. In these circumstances 'a fundamental rethinking of the nature of the state' is what must come first (*FEER*, 18 June, 1992 (letter)). The rest of this chapter must then be largely concerned with ideas and initiatives readily applicable only in liberal democracies. Yet in three ways not yet discussed corruption control features in both Marxist and non-Marxist states and in the processes of régime change and demise. Corruption control had a conspicuous yet unsuccessful - perhaps ultimately counterproductive - place on the agenda in most communist countries in Europe in the 1980s and a strong presence in informed popular opinion. Whatever its role was, it was more than its superficial appearance: thus on one view it sought to cement an alliance between the élite and the masses against the allegedly corrupt bureaucracy in circumstances of decaying political legitimacy (Holmes, 1993, 42). The attempt failed and in fact public indignation at political corruption, élite and bureaucratic rather than petty and everyday, was one element in the collapse of Soviet and satellite communism in the 1980s. Political corruption remains a problem in the successor states but it is now recognised for what it is and the political conditions necessary for its control now exist. In the other communist heartland, Wing Lo (1993) demonstrates that corruption control began primarily as a version of class struggle and even in its later antibureaucratic version was commonly no more than a weapon for the pursuit of factional interests. Nevertheless popular feeling on the issue was one element in the events of Tiananmen Square (Holmes, 1993, 8). It may yet have a role as a precipitant of political change driven from below.

In the third world régime changes commonly appear yet more closely connected to corruption, to popular concern, and also to politicians' or generals' seizure upon the issue as a rationale or slogan for their actions. In practice one corrupt régime is almost invariably in such circumstances succeeded by another: change has been essentially superficial, of persons or parties rather than of methods and morality, and corruption remains evident and entrenched. As its place on the political agenda was cosmetic so control of corruption, real though it is as an issue, remains elusive and ephemeral.

Thirdly the concept of 'islands of integrity', advocated by Transparency International and piloted in Ecuador, can be simply stated as the providing (and later extending) of enclaves of honesty in a territory of corruption by incorporating every player into a well monitored agreement not to bribe. Honest leadership is the key to success.

Discussion of corruption control in the more practical and policy oriented sense remains nevertheless for the most part concerned with the liberal democracies and especially with the USA where at federal, state and local levels political corruption has been a major concern for some two centuries but where also anti-corruption measures have had some success. Gardiner and Lyman (1978, 126-35) note that in one area where such measures have succeeded personal integrity and a strong participatory element in the political and administrative system are ranked by observers as the principal element in effective controls. This is to reassert the primacy of political morality discussed earlier in this chapter. The system of government is ranked second and preventive measures third. It has already been noted that confusion and incompetence foster corruption and so an emphasis on good government in this context, even in second place, occasions no surprise. Good government has important geographical components: accessibility, a clear and certain spatial and hierarchical structure (rather than any particular degree or form of centralisation or decentralisation). Others are controversial, the frequent movement of public servants to avoid prolonged residence in one place or responsibility for one issue, the minimalisation of regulation.

The most extended practical discussion of corruption control, albeit in a particular context, occurs in chapters 9 to 13 of Amick's *The American Way of Graft* (1976) and the chapter headings indicate its scope: 'Running a tight ship'; 'Eliminating the arbitrary decision'; 'Avenues of appeal'; 'No compromising connections'; 'Sunlight on the system'. (Chapter 14 closes the book with discussion of an honesty ethic in public life.) Land-use provides most of the examples, unsurprisingly so given the author's tacit support for Paul's assertion that 'zoning is the single biggest corruptor of the nation's local government' (*NYT*, 13 May 1975). Among Amick's proposals in this context, clearly more widely applicable when translated into principles, are: a single code and agency within any single jurisdiction for land-use regulation; its professional administration according to prescribed and public procedures under the general direction of an elected group (tax, licensing and franchises are proposed for similar treatment); explicit decision criteria (some cases where corruption is suspected turn out to be caused by unpublicised changes in the rules - openness and publicity help the bureaucrat as well as the citizen); expeditious appeals procedures focused on key issues and avoiding *de novo* hearings which are a common cause of delay; and full financial disclosure by officials and companies and, especially important in the United States planning context, by secret land trusts often used to conceal true ownership and suspected of corrupt activity.

The essential flavour of Amick's argument and programme is clear: honesty first, then openness, orderliness and professionalism. He is also aware that graft resistance rather than graft proofing is all that can be reasonably expected (Amick, 1976, 161). Two years later and even more particularly in a North American land-use planning context Gardiner and Lyman (1978) argue for very similar measures and provide extended exemplification ranging from the extremely to the negligibly corrupt. They suggest simple policies visibly implemented, good records, disclosure of interest, review of decisions.

A third world perspective provided by Wade (1984, 39-40), in what is probably a much more difficult situation, is much more pragmatic. He notes in the Indian irrigation context that frequent transfers of irrigation engineers, a lucrative calling for the dishonest, was the British counter-corruption strategy but that this no longer works. He proposes less frequent and seemingly more random movement managed by committees rather than individuals. Hope (1987) more systematically argues for deconcentration of decision taking to lower levels, devolution of authority to lower level authorities, delegation to public enterprise, and privatisation, in most respects an approach sympathetic to the political fashions of the 1980s but by no means devoid of practical insights. Nevertheless the case for an element of central control is often made.

Different problems demand different remedies but in effect the same underlying rationale, of orderly, open and accessible government. This equates with the 'corruption proofing' of the process of government implicitly proposed by many commentators if explicitly by few. Klitgaard whose 1988 book *Controlling Corruption* is one of very few directly on the topic argues for government programmes and procedures to receive a vulnerability assessment as is already the case with US Office of Management and Budget 'Internal Control Guidelines' (84-5). Two years earlier an Australian cabinet minister floated the idea of 'crime impact statements' for legislation and regulations (Bottom, 1987, 107), evidently with corruption in mind and probably proceeding from analogy with the environmental impact statement. The probable implications of any law or rule in the area of corruption would thus be aired and considered at an early stage. (Ironically the minister's career later foundered on the shoal of corruption charges (*The Bulletin*, 16 February 1988).) The idea can be traced back at least to the early 1960s and the writings of McMullen (1961).

There remain to be discussed a number of specific policy areas, areas important in the eyes of the public and certainly not to be dismissed or discounted simply because many authorities rank them after integrity and system. For here, even among deliberately contrived failures (and loads of whitewash) are to be found practical solutions.

Whistle blowing

Currently conspicuous among these is the 'whistle blower' (note once more the role of analogy - but is it of policeman or referee?), in other words the role of the honest and well informed insider and his or her sense of outrage. Traditionally the 'whistle blower' has occupied dangerous and uncertain ground, unpopular not only with those informed upon but also more generally within the organisation, and often subject even as or after irregularities are exposed to formal punishment. Three-quarters of a sample of New South Wales public servants, working in a state where corruption is a significant issue, believed that those who report corruption are likely to suffer as a consequence (Gorta and Forell, 1995, 335). The problem is to reconcile his or her most useful and legitimate role with the reasonable demand for loyalty within an organisation and with the fact that wild and unfounded accusations are often made to draw attention to the accuser (Cooper and Wright, 1992, 225-6). There is some evidence that whistle blowers who see corruption as a problem of individual morality are more likely to receive public support than those who view it as systemic (Cooper and Wright, 1992, 319-20). The usefulness of the whistle blower is recognised and several countries are moving legislatively to protect his or her position, but the scope of this particular control measure is obviously limited. What will always be needed however is witnesses after the event and they will require similar protection. The wider role of the whistle blower as a source of information as to what actually goes on is too easily forgotten.

Official action

The typical governmental response to accusations of corruption is, usually with reluctance, to set up some form of enquiry or, as initially in the New Zealand-Cook Islands tax fraud case - the ongoing Wine Box enquiry as it is known - to permit an existing body to investigate. This action does not in itself vouchsafe the government's anti-corruption credentials: it may be obstructive in all sorts of ways from terms of reference to reluctance to take action. Committees can evade some of these obstacles, the Santharam Committee for example, but they are necessarily subject in the last resort to the reluctance of government to act. In the Santharam instance the government tried to exclude political graft as opposed to administrative corruption from the committee's explorations. The committee found a legal way round this obstacle but subsequent legislation restricted the role of vigilance committees to the administrative area (Dwivedy and Bhargava, 1967, 29-31). From the scholarly perspective what matters is that even in hostile circumstances, in West Africa (Arlin, 1976, 66) for example, official enquiries have exposed a great deal of evidence. They have had much more success here than in achieving control; Ghana's 109 commissions of this kind between 1957 and 1990 are not generally regarded as the reason why it is now usually regarded as by African standards only moderately corrupt (Ayittey, 1990, 167). They also serve, whatever the preferences of politicians, to keep the issue in the public eye. For this reason their role is probably more effective if they are occasional and high profile.

There is however also a place for the standing or permanent committee of enquiry, the public watchdog, even though many of the preceding arguments suggesting the probability of limited success hold good. At worst the anticorruption agency is itself corrupted. However the Hong Kong Independent Committee Against Corruption (ICAC) (Lethbridge, 1985) has been evidently effective, though possibly at a price in terms of public service efficiency, creativity and expedition. Its success rate in the courts, where such cases are not easily proved, is about seventy per cent. A more recent counterpart, the New South Wales ICAC, was set up in 1988 (Temby, 1990) in a state with a long history of corruption reaching to the very highest (i.e. cabinet) levels. Its aim is as much investigative as punitive and it also emphasises corruption proofing the system. In this case the problem of how genuine is the political will has been addressed, not necessarily solved, by making the body answerable to the legislature rather than the minister. (Whatever its success corruption, notably of the police, remains a conspicuous problem in New South Wales.) Elsewhere in Australia the question of political will remains an issue in this agency context, currently in Queensland, also a state with a long history of corruption, and one which has attracted attention in the national media (*The Australian*, 28-29 September 1996). Finally the small proportion of all complaints to such bodies deemed worth following up deserves comment, about 1 in 15 in Malaysia in the early 1980s. Even allowing for the certainty of imperfections in any agency the figure is low, its main basis being the public propensity to exaggerate and to bring malicious cases. About half of the cases followed up ended in conviction (*FEER*, 2 April 1987). Even if Malaysian procedures are extremely selective as to what is pursued the figures indicate one problem area for legislators seeking to protect whistle blowers, the presence of the few genuine and often very important cases set in a matrix of the imaginary, the malicious, the absurd, and the unproven.

The media

A much older and generally more effective vehicle and tradition of corruption exposure - leading to control - is the freedom of the press and the activities of journalists. To these may be added the more general and more recent concept of freedom of information legislation. To them the scholar turns for both example and evidence. In the specific context of control their capacity to turn issues and events into scandal, to generate an 'active sense of outrage', to rouse public awareness and indignation has been regarded as of critical importance. In terms of their task this capacity is however secondary to the business of getting the news - not all corruption is newsworthy - and publishing it. This is not in principle a very different task from that of the researcher, but in the case of corruption the journalist is usually more practically trained and better resourced. Difficulties remain for him or her: few journalists are able to work solely on cases of corruption; daily deadlines conflict with the need for months or years of investigation; legal as well as political systems vary in their support for and tolerance of investigative journalism (Ayittey, 1990, 177-8 and 215); media owners may suppress such investigations because of their own position or at the behest of advertisers. They may, as happened to me in one case, refuse to publish letters seeking to enlist public help and to gain information. Nor are journalists entirely innocent: corruption is reportedly endemic in India's financial press (*FEER*, 5 October 1995) on the basis of direct bribery. The weak investigative tradition of the Japanese media (van Wolferen, 1990, 93-100) is often cited as one of the causes of endemic political corruption. Similarly the French press of the inter-war period was notably corruptible, ultimately a reflexion upon its proprietors (Jeanneney, 1982, 237-68). In general terms corrupt government requires and uses corrupt media whether the corruption is focused at the proprietorial, editorial, or reporting levels. On the other hand newspaper exposure of corruption played a part in the defeat of Congress in India's 1989 election (*NYT*, 3 December 1991).

The media have few rivals in the effective exposure of corruption and thus a central role in its control. Public ambivalence towards investigative reporting is encapsulated in the term 'muck raking'.

Originally taken from Bunyan's *Pilgrim's Progress* it was applied descriptively and supportively and critically to the writers who exposed municipal corruption in North American cities in the second half of last century. It is now used even more loosely, ambivalently and even derogatorily, as in Bunyan's original use. One obvious reason is the use of the same methods for less worthy ends. The phrase certainly summarises the task. This book owes much to conversations with Brian Priestley, formerly of the *Birmingham Evening Mail*, whose most successful investigation in the field of corruption led to the jailing of a county chairman on planning corruption charges.

The media will not always be popular or right in this context but their role is essential. The ordinary citizen is by comparison poorly placed. His or her experience is usually as a victim on the down side of an unequal relationship. Nor is the citizen trained or resourced to take even evasive, let alone investigative, action. And the difficult position of the whistle blower has already been discussed.

Legal process

Finally there is the question of legal process, of the role of police and more generally of the law. Recall again Alatas' observation that good laws are not in short supply, but good leaders are (Alatas, 1990, 59-60). No legal code affirms corruption, but evidently some are, by accident or design, more tolerant than others. It must however be noted that bribes are often deductible for tax purposes: France and Norway do not even require evidence that they have been paid! Proposals for change often meet resistance from the business community (*European*, 18-24 April 1996). Judicial bribery and corruption remains not unknown, notably in the United States, but more generally it is observed that endemic low and middle level corruption can be accompanied by an honest judiciary as was the case in imperial India and remains to a degree in much of the contemporary third world. The reverse would rarely be true: corrupt judges create a corrupt society. Lawyers have played a leading role in the campaign against political corruption and in a variety of roles, but it is interesting and disturbing to note that a broad interest over the profession as a whole is paralleled by considerable disinterest among commercial lawyers. Honest judges and lawyers at work on corruption cases are confronted with issues which at least in the past have arisen infrequently and where acquittals are common. For the latter the reason is simply that the nature of the corrupt process makes it hard to obtain the necessary standard of proof.

What then is the place of geography in a discussion of cures and controls? Firstly there is no right geographical answer, no bureaucratic geography, no spatial organisation of the police or judicial apparatus which guarantees success. But it is equally the case that a bad geography in the broader sense of an ill conceived administrative framework will be conducive to corruption in its generation of delay, uncertainty and conflict. Good administrative geographies at every scale from global to local - a deliberate plural - will help. Secondly a great deal of what has been written about this aspect of corruption derives from the planning process, especially in the USA, though it appears to have a wider applicability. Land-use and its management, a central concern of geographical scholarship and the profession of many geographers, dominates empirical experience of not only the phenomenon but of its resolution in much of the west and is not insignificant more widely. This has implications for geographers' investigations of the planning process and for the education of geographers (and others) as planners which are too often ignored. Thirdly place attributes have a role in shaping the climate of control. Most existing tax havens of dubious repute (Switzerland is an exception) are very small countries, not a few are still formal dependencies, with very modest resource bases the economies of which have grown to depend on the finance sector and not just the least reputable part. Can corruption control target the corrupt while allowing for the maintenance of the legitimate element in the finance sector and without unduly infringing national sovereignty?

It is much easier to provide an orderly account of corruption control, even of prospective cures, than to be optimistic or cheerful. This is not an area of conspicuous contemporary success. In much of the world the structure of government, not necessarily the popular mood, facilitates corruption to the point of inevitability even when the élites are themselves honest. Understanding how corruption works is necessary for its control but it is no guarantee that good policy will be effectively implemented. A central control issue is always how to circumvent the power of influential and determined beneficiaries. The second aspect, that of 'moral change' is even less clear in its features and more contentious in its application. One of the most famous recent enquiries by Fitzgerald in Queensland into corruption summarises both features and difficulties of this dimension: 'corruption takes root in money and power which are always present. Its extent depends on the social environment. In some environments, it flourishes into a tangled wilderness; in others, its growth is inhibited and perhaps it can even be eradicated. Minimum requirements include ethical leadership, an informed community, a generally open and honest society, and efficient methods of detection followed by hard punishment - a tall order.' (Dickie, 1988, 244).

11 Afterthoughts: the future of political corruption

Both the scholarly and the practical versions of enquiry into political corruption rarely venture into speculation as to the likely course of events either in particular cases or in such broad terms as probable levels and forms of incidence ten or twenty years hence. Such discussion is rarely on the agenda, not least because it conflicts in its necessarily speculative character with the norms and mores of the social sciences from which most investigators are drawn. Nevertheless the future has a place in scholarship and most appropriately in the concluding chapter of a book which seeks to heighten intellectual awareness and to bring about an increase in scholarly activity. One preliminary comment is therefore to express the hope and belief that political corruption will gain a position which is more central and more conspicuous on the agenda of a number of disciplines than is at present the case, even if that place is an account of its declining significance. However a more dismal but not unrealistic assumption is that the phenomenon of political corruption will still be widespread and significant, that any battle will by then be no more than half won and that any campaign will be difficult and drawn out. There is no equivalent in this context of the magic bullet. In any event I share with most other writers the view that both the human and the political condition contain a number of durable components which rule out the idea of cure and that therefore our attention should rather be focused upon control at the lowest possible level of incidence.

As political corruption is created in and by context it is also appropriate once more to draw attention to those several contexts. What happens to corruption will be in a large part a reflexion of the quality of government: political corruption is enfeebled by good government (in all its diversity) and engendered by bad government. Do we expect the world to be better or worse governed in a generation from now? Is there any evidence that government is getting better or worse at a variety of scales? The same is true of economic conditions, not only in terms of wealth but more importantly in terms of social justice. 'Fair shares for all' is a good bulwark against corruption provided however that the pie is of adequate size. In both these categories the evidence is a matter for contention and debate, and as far as corruption itself is concerned our argument is taken back to the fundamental problem of that evidence in its relationship to the uncertain totality of the phenomenon. We do not know how much of the resurgence of political corruption, in France for example, is real increase, how much is heightened awareness, and how much remains concealed. What we may be reasonably certain of is that France (or even Italy) is less corrupt than Zaire or Cambodia, and that the lesser levels of corruption both derive from and contribute to better government and a stronger economy in the former instances. Our questions however remain: has France entered a period of deteriorating political honesty? is it conceivable that Zaire will cease to be a synonym for apparently hopeless and endemic political corruption?

All four of the examples used above provide some grounds for pessimism, the most basic of which is the prevalence of the phenomenon. Something as big as this will not disappear or substantially diminish in a short period of time. The pessimist will then point to the extent and forms of political corruption in many third world countries, some of the largest and potentially wealthiest among them, Nigeria for example; to its resurgence in the former communist countries as indicative of a malaise not peculiar to their particular political experience; and to the recognition that it is almost ubiquitous in the western democracies - as it always has been - and that some of that present recognition resembles resurgence. The essence of this argument is that political corruption is on the ascendant, after perhaps a century and a half of retreat, and that this is likely to continue.

The pessimists' case however is more than a matter of assessing and evaluating empirical evidence. It can also be developed on more theoretical bases even if they are to be related, in the context of this chapter's concerns, both backwards and forwards into the real world. Four such bases may be summarised as: the market, the decline of community, waning political confidence, and the rise of the lobby. Firstly a feature of the political order during the last two decades in much of the western world (the ex-communist states now included) has been the waning fortunes of Keynesian interventionism and the waxing fortunes of a belief in the efficacy of market forces. While it would be a perverse and twisted logic which interpreted a belief in the market as an inevitable breeding ground for corruption - and inasmuch as it frequently operates via deregulation the reverse case can be made - yet in its emphasis on user payment for services or more crudely 'you can have it if you can pay for it' this position readily degenerates into an environment favourable for corruption. In some quarters the simultaneous move away from an emphasis on community rights and responsibilities to an emphasis upon the individual - to the extent in some cases of abandonment of any concept of community - would be viewed in similar terms. The individual must look after him or herself and as the community does not exist so it cannot be damaged by actions traditionally deemed corrupt which are therefore harmless. Again the argument that individualism leads to corruption is not a wholly convincing or overwhelming one, but the idea that where the individual is called on to look after his or her own interests - since no one else will - then some diminution of acceptance of the political rules, formal and informal, may be expected to follow has some power. The end point of individualisation is then the disappearance of meaning from the concept of the political and thus of political corruption: conversely concepts of public good and community feature frequently in discussions of political corruption, and are taken for granted, perhaps too readily so, by those who regard corruption as a malevolent force.

The third ground for pessimism, not unrelated to the above and occupying a similar time frame, is an alleged collapse in public confidence in politicians and political institutions. They do not enjoy as much popular respect as they did a generation ago, in part on the grounds of their diminished capacity or willingness to deliver the goods. There is therefore an increased willingness to explore ways of circumventing the system. (The resemblance to what happened in communist Europe is evident.) One among several possible explanations is particularly relevant in the context of corruption, the belief that political institutions have fallen more and more into the hands of those interested primarily in power - even just power for its own sake - and away from those driven by such forces as principle and service. Recall Acton's famous words. Furthermore the elements of consensus politics evident in many of the democracies a generation ago - and perhaps vestigially then present in communist states - have given way to a polarisation in which substantial minorities see themselves as no longer merely, and they would hope temporarily, disadvantaged but as victims of policy changes which are certainly in no wise consensual but designed for their permanent and irreversible disbenefit. An important secondary dimension of this argument is the growing power of the central element of government (and especially of the executive element) at the expense of the local (and perhaps also the legislative), the loss of community power and the growth of remote - and thus often practically delayed - and insensitive central authority. In these circumstances a loss of public political confidence is unsurprising and a quest for alternatives - of which corruption is but one - likely. Workable decentralised government remains a powerful check on corruption. This appears to be an effective approach in some third world situations, Uganda and Tanzania for example. It is however evidently not the whole story in the third world, except inasmuch as the term political confidence can be applied to the predictability of colonial rule. Third world corruption is widely regarded as cause rather than consequence of a loss in political confidence, as one of the obstacles to be overcome in the process of political development. Such an interpretation is not however without wider significance, in Italy for example.

Lobbying has always happened and the question of its legitimate limits is of long standing. However the increased role, presence and sophistication of the lobbying process - and its stage army of consultants - is a fourth ground for pessimistic concern, already discussed at length in chapter seven. The effect is to enhance the role and power of the advocate, and to make it more likely that he or she will go beyond reasonable persuasion in the quest for advantage: recall Lippman's definition of corruption as the 'traffic in privileges'.

All of these arguments can be presented at a variety of levels from the sophisticated to the naïve. Their effect will depend not upon their intellectual validity but upon their popular credibility; political institutions for example do not have to fail but rather to be thought to be failing for alternatives to be sought. The restoration of confidence in government and belief in community however it might happen will have more effect than scholarly refutation of any of the positions discussed above. The diminution of corruption is firstly a practical and only secondly an intellectual exercise.

There remain to be considered however, again in context, the not inconsiderable grounds for optimism, for while the battle may never be won yet there are reasonable grounds for expecting durable improvement. The first among these relates back to the empirical argument which leads off the pessimists' case. While the evidence may be used in this way it can equally be interpreted as a destruction of the functionalist case with its almost inevitable argument of transience. In much of the world, especially the third world, corruption delivers the goods if at all in a manifestly unsatisfactory way and shows no signs of giving way or leading into a better situation. And as the assault on the functionalists' position makes very clear, acceptance of a lasting and beneficial role for corruption carries with it some very strange ideas as to moral values. In other words our present understanding of political corruption provides a strong intellectual foundation and justification for action. Without action things will not improve and the phenomenon will not simply die away.

The intellectual collapse of the functionalist defence has been accompanied by a diminution in whatever popular appeal it ever possessed. Whenever and wherever there is the opportunity freely to express an opinion on the matter the vast majority favours honest government. This does not mean that individuals will not try to outwit the system in particular cases and nor does it deny the hypocrisy of at least a sizeable minority - often the most powerful and the most practically corrupt - but it does express the basic preference of most men and women for honest government. The articulation and implementation of this philosophy, supported as it is at least in principle by most constitutions and legal and religious systems, is another matter. The individual is usually in a weak position, not least as whistle blower, and institutions designed to counter corruption where they are not merely cosmetic are rarely user friendly at the citizen level. Mass movements to counter corruption are a rarity, though the issue can figure in their plans, of Poland's Solidarity for example, and are only too easily manipulated or taken over by groups with other priorities. The most optimistic development in this area is Transparency International. Interestingly its initial focus on one particular kind of corruption, that in international business, has broadened out into a wider concern for good honest and open government in such dimensions as press freedom, judicial independence, and parliamentary control of the executive. However it seems unlikely that it can develop the popular appeal of say Amnesty International, its closest cousin. Note too that whereas Amnesty operates from outside the area it wishes to change Transparency International must work from within and is thus much more vulnerable to criticism, attempted manipulation and even apathy than its counterpart. The fact remains that Transparency International has, given the relative complexity of its concerns, proved remarkably successful, especially in the mobilisation of civil society against corruption. The enthusiasm generated by its visitations - and perhaps also its occasional confrontations with governments - indicate both that there is extensive popular concern and support for its aims and that the issues with which it deals are of serious concern in many countries.

Earlier in this chapter the possibility that the broad cultural environment of the 1990s might be seen to engender a pessimistic prognosis through such matters as elevation of the status of the market and the individual was discussed. This environment is not however uniformly or ubiquitously unfavourable. Anyone working in a large organisation will instantly recognise the word 'accountability' as an important contemporary restatement of an older philosophy which had lost much of its way and momentum. The same can be said of 'quality assurance'. Twenty years hence we will be able to decide whether or not they were mere fashions or catch phrases as opposed to matters of substance. But at least in principle their existence and promotion is grounds for optimism. Neither is compatible with political corruption, and their implementation ought to generate its reduction. In this context the emphasis placed by many governments on service delivery, and its measurement, is a helpful sign, providing weapons for the communities and individuals who are not getting what they need - and have paid for - because of the intervention of corruption. The World Bank has pursued this line. There is however an obvious risk in both the areas of accountability and quality assurance which risks lie within the practical experience of many individuals, that accountability and quality control will be achieved on the basis not of simplicity but of complex structures, tendentious criteria and time consuming processes. If accountability and quality control are not to foster that corruption which they ought to diminish then their implementation must be simple, appropriate and expeditious. Sadly that is by no means always the case.

As to the prospective usefulness of the characterisations displayed and discussed in chapter four, none have lost their usefulness and who can tell what insights have yet to be encapsulated in this way? A choice among them, with an eye to the future, is necessarily subjective and personal. I would mention three among the many. Acton has lost neither force nor discernment. The control of corruption necessitates the regulation of the use of political and administrative power. At the very least the tendency - a word so often forgotten when the dictum is quoted - signals a rule of thumb for the honest political manager. Be on your guard! Secondly the pathological analogy most adequately among all such covers the several dimensions of political corruption, more so than such closely related terms as disease, pollution and parasitism. In particular it accommodates the fact that political corruption exists within the body politic, generating deformity and even adaptation while yet, and especially at the superficial level, allowing survival. Finally Rosenthal's restatement of the congressional perspective of 1977, corruption as erosion of competition in business, deserves reiteration in a period when multinational business is an increasingly powerful (and often corrupt) political force. Perhaps however the word corrosion is an even more apt description given the covert character of corruption, its location within working systems, and the eventual catastrophic consequences.

There are reasons for believing in the possibility of a real diminution in the incidence of political corruption over the next twenty years. Since however the expansion of corruption is an insidious and invisible process reactive to changing conditions in both the real world and our evaluation of it, so its diminution calls for imaginative and proactive reactions. How the insights of accountability, quality control and, to introduce a third issue risk management, are handled is one of these. Another, raised in the body of this book, is the idea of corruption proofing (implicit in which is an audit process) as applicable to all legislation and regulation, a formidable task especially given its retrospective component, but the surest way of guaranteeing progress.

Progress is of course an unfashionable, even a politically and intellectually incorrect, word but I am left in no doubt that it is the most appropriate word which can be applied to any successful action of corruption control. Save at the most trivial level corruption does nothing for human happiness and weighed in the balance of costs and benefits it is disastrously and divisively wanting. 'Mene mene tekel upharsin' (Daniel, 5, v25). The intellectual judgement has been made: the vital task is its practical implementation.

Appendix

A letter to a newspaper and a response.

This letter appeared in an English provincial newspaper in 1993. (It was rejected for publication by another.) It generated a modest but rewarding response. The second letter, one of those responses, appears indicative of a widespread attitude and perception.

I am writing to enlist the help of your readers in a research project which I am undertaking while on sabbatical leave from the University of Canterbury, New Zealand.

Worldwide, the question of political integrity is increasingly discussed as a central issue in human well-being, for the individual, the community, the nation and the world.

More particularly the use of illegal payments, cash or kind, to get round the law or administrative procedures, seems to have become so important a part of the political process as to require not only more action from law enforcement agencies but more research from the scholarly community.

Of course "bribery and corruption", to use the good old-fashioned term, is nothing new; it may not even be on the increase. But recognition of the need for research into the topic certainly is much more recent.

I would therefore be interested to hear from any of your readers who believe they are aware of situations of this kind, of what they would allege to be political corruption, going on in this locality now or in the recent past; also from those who in their working life or travels encountered political corruption, especially any who were involved in attempts to eliminate it.

The topic is an extremely sensitive one and, of course, my choice of this region does not imply a belief that it is particularly corrupt: the reverse is almost certainly the case.

As I find your letter rather unusual I would like to say. Anyone intelligent in G Britain has not far to look for political corruption these days. The present government refuses to tax wealthy people, landowners, farmers etc soley, to keep their vote.

In fact they give them tax-payers free handouts running into hundreds of millions annualy. This country is not poor if the billions that have escaped loop-holes were unearthed. And the Common Market is the biggest fraud to enrich wealthy persons at the expence of the poor of the World. You might not class my comments as corruption, but they are as clear as daylight robbery.

Bibliography

Acton, J.E.D-A. (Lord Acton) (1956), *Essays on Freedom and Power*, Thames and Hudson, London. (A selection by G. Himmelfarb.)

Ahmad, Z.H. and Crouch, H. (eds) (1985), *Military and Civilian Relations in South-East Asia*, Oxford, Singapore.

Alatas, S.H. (1990), *Corruption: its nature, causes and functions*, Gower, Aldershot. (The best modern introduction.)

Alatas, S.H. (1993), 'Corruption', in *Oxford Companion to the Politics of the World*, Oxford, New York, pp. 198-9.

Alexander, H.E. and Caiden, G.E. (eds) (1985), *The Politics and Economics of Organized Crime*, Gower, Aldershot.

Amick, G. (1976), *The American Way of Graft*, Centre for the Analysis of Public Issues, Princeton.

Andreski, S. (1966), *Parasitism and Subversion: the case of Latin America*, Weidenfeld and Nicholson, London.

Andvig, J.C. (1995), 'Corruption in the North Sea oil industry: issues and assessments', *Crime, Law and Social Change*, vol. 23, pp. 289-313.

Anechiarico, F. and Jacobs, J.B. (1995), 'Panopticism and financial controls: the anti-corruption project in public administration', *Crime, Law and Social Change*, vol. 22, pp. 361-79.

Anon (1976), 'The cement racket', in *Africa Guide 1977*, Africa Guide Co., Saffron Walden, pp. 213-23.

Anon (probably Mugford, S.) (1981), 'Editorial: the place of corruption in advanced societies', *Australian and New Zealand Journal of Criminology*, vol. 14, pp. 193-6.

Arlin, K. (1976), 'Bribery and Corruption in West Africa', in *Africa Guide 1977*, Africa Guide Co., Saffron Walden, pp. 66-7.

Armah, A.K. (1969), *The Beautiful Ones are not yet Born*, Penguin (African Writers Series), London.

The Australian (1964-), Sydney.

Ayittey, G.B.N. (1992), *Africa Betrayed*, St Martin's, New York.

Bailey, J. (1988), *Governing Mexico: the statecraft of crisis management*, Macmillan, London.

Bandyopadhyay, S. (1987), *Burma Today*, Papyrus, Calcutta.

Banfield, E.C. (1958), *The Moral Basis of a Backward Society*, Research Center in Economic Development and Cultural Change (Chicago), Free Press, Glencoe.

Barlow, H.D. (1993), 'From fiddle factors to network of collusion: charting the waters of small business crime', *Crime, Law and Social Change*, vol. 20, pp. 319-37.

Bayart, J-F. (1989), *L'Etat en Afrique: la politique du ventre*, Fayart, Paris.

Benson, G.C.S. (1978), *Political corruption in America*, Lexington, Lexington.

Bhagwati, J.N. (ed) (1974), *Illegal Transactions in International Trade: theory and measurement*, Elsevier, New York.

Bok, S. (1978), *Lying: moral choice in public and private life*, Harvester, Hassocks.

Bok, S. (1984), *Secrets: concealment and revelation*, Oxford, Oxford.

Bottom, B. (1987), *Connections II: crime rackets and networks of influence in Australia*, Sun Books, South Melbourne.

Bottom, B. et al. (1991), *Inside Victoria: a chronicle of scandal*, Pan, Chippendale N.S.W.

Brabainti, R. (1962), 'Reflections on bureaucratic corruption', *Public Administration*, vol. 40, pp. 357-72.

Braginsky, S. (1996), 'Corruption and Schumpeterian growth in different economic environments', *Contemporary Economic Policy*, vol. 14, pp. 14-25.

Braithwaite, J., Grabovsky, P. and Rickwood, D. (1986), 'Research note: corruption allegations and Australian business regulation', *Australian and New Zealand Journal of Criminology*, vol. 19, pp. 179-86.

Bretton, H. (1973), *Power and Politics in Africa*, Longman, London.

Brumberg, A. (ed) (1983), *Poland: genesis of a revolution*, Vintage, New York.

The Bulletin (1880-), Sydney.

Caiden, G.E. (1988), 'Towards a general theory of official corruption', *Asian Journal of Public Administration*, vol. 10, pp. 3-26.

Callow, A.B. (1966), *The Tweed Ring*, Oxford, New York.

Calvert, S. and Calvert, P. (1989), *Argentina: political culture and instability*, Macmillan, London.

Camp, R.A. (1992), *Generals in the Palacio: the military in modern Mexico*, Macmillan, London.

Cannon, M. (1966), *The Land Boomers*, Melbourne University, Melbourne.

Carino, L.V. (ed) (1986), *Bureaucratic Corruption in Asia: causes, consequences and controls*, JMC Press, Manila.

Caro, R.A. (1974), *The Power Broker: Robert Moses and the fall of New York*, Knopf, New York.

Cecil, H. (1964), *Tipping the Scales*, Hutchinson, London.

Chambliss, W.J. (1978), *On the take: from petty crooks to presidents*, Indiana University, Bloomington.

Charlton, R. (1990), 'Exploring the byways of African political corruption: Botswana and deviant case analysis', *Corruption and Reform*, vol. 5, pp. 1-28.

Cheung, S.N.S. (1996), 'Simplistic general equilibrium theory of corruption', *Contemporary Economic Policy*, vol. 14, pp. 1-5.

Chibnall, S. and Saunders, P. (1977), 'Worlds apart: notes on the social reality of corruption', *British Journal of Sociology*, vol. 28, pp. 138-54.

Chubb, J. and Vannicelli, M. (1988), 'Italy: a web of scandals in a flawed democracy', in Markovits, A.S. and Silverstein, M. (eds), *The politics of scandal: power and process in liberal democracies*, Holmes and Meier, New York, pp. 122-50.

Clark, D. (1988), 'Recent literature on corruption', *Asian Journal of Public Administration*, vol. 10, pp. 20-5.

Clark, G.L. and Dear, M. (1984), *State Apparatus: structures and language of legitimacy*, Allen and Unwin, Boston.

Clarke, M. (ed) (1983), *Corruption: causes, consequences and control*, Pinter, London.

Coaldrake, P. (1989), *Working the system: government in Queensland*, University of Queensland, St Lucia.

Cockcroft, L. (1990), *Africa's Way: a journey from the past*, Tauris, London.

Cohen, S.B. and Rosenthal, L.D. (1971), 'A geographical model for political systems analysis', *Geographical Review*, vol. 61, pp. 5-31.

Coker Commission (1962), *Report of the Coker Commission of Inquiry into the affairs of certain statutory corporations in Western Nigeria* (4 vols), Ibadan.

Cooper, T.L. and Wright, N.D. (eds) (1992), *Exemplary Public Administrators: character and leadership in government*, Jossey-Bass, San Francisco.

Corruption and Reform (1986-92), Kluwer, Dordrecht. (Thereafter incorporated into *Crime, Law and Social Change*.)

Crime, Law and Social Change (1977-), Kluwer, Dordrecht. (From 1993 incorporates *Corruption and Reform*.)

Current, R.N. (1976), *History of Wisconsin (volume 2),* 'The Civil War Era 1848-73', Wisconsin State Historical Society, Madison.

Curtis, G.L. (1988), *The Japanese Way of Politics*, Columbia University, New York.

Darby, H.C. (1962), 'The problem of geographical description', *Institute of British Geographers: Transactions and Papers*, vol. 30, pp. 1-14.

Davidson, B. (1992), *The Black Man's Burden: Africa and the curse of the nation state*, Times, New York.

de Soto, H. (1989), *The Other Path: the invisible revolution in the third world*, Harper and Row, New York.

Dickie, P. (1988), *The Road to Fitzgerald*, University of Queensland, St Lucia.

Djilas, M. (1957), *The New Class: an analysis of the communist system*, Thames and Hudson, London.

Doig, A. (1984), *Corruption and misconduct in contemporary British politics*, Pelican, London.

Dumont, R. and Mazoyer, M. (1969), *Développement et Socialismes*, Seuil, Paris.

Dwivedy, S. and Bhargava, G.S. (1967), *Political corruption in India*, Popular Book Services, New Delhi.

Earle, J. (1975), *Italy in the 1970s*, David and Charles, Newton Abbot.

The Economist (1843-), London.

Eigen, P. (1993), 'Transparency International - the coalition against corruption in international business transactions', *Development and Cooperation* (German Foundation for International Development, Bonn), vol. 13, pp. 9-12.

Eisenstadt, A.S., Hoogenboom, A. and Trefousse, H.L. (1978), *Before Watergate: problems of corruption in American society*, Brooklyn College Press, New York.

Eisenstadt, S.N. and Leonardhand, R. (1981), *Political Clientelism, Patronage and Development*, Sage, Beverly Hills. (Volume 3 of *Contemporary Political Sociology*.)

Ekeh, P.P. (1975), 'Colonialism and the two publics: a theoretical statement', *Comparative Studies in Society and History*, vol. 17, pp. 91-112.

Elwert, G. (1993), 'The law of venal accumulation: corruption in Africa', *Development and Cooperation* (German Foundation for International Development, Bonn), vol. 13, pp. 16-18.

Engels, B. (1993), 'Is good governance possible?', *Development and Cooperation* (German Foundation for International Development, Bonn), vol. 13, pp. 13-16.

European, The (1990-), London.

Far Eastern Economic Review (1946-), Hong Kong.

Fehér, F., Heller, A. and Márkus, G. (1983), *Dictatorship Over Needs*, Basil Blackwell, Oxford.

Financial Times (1892-), London. (The fullest treatment of the subject in any quality UK newspaper.)

Fitch, B. and Oppenheimer, M. (1966), *Ghana: end of an illusion*, Monthly Review Press, London and New York.

Ford, H.J. (1904), 'Municipal corruption: review of Lincoln Steffens, The Shame of the Cities', *Political Science Quarterly*, vol. 19, pp. 673-86.

Fox, J. (1992), *The Politics of Food in Mexico: state power and social mobilization*, Cornell University, Ithaca.

Friedrich, C.J. (1974), *The Pathology of Politics: violence, betrayal, corruption, secrecy and propaganda*, Harper and Row, New York.

Furlong, P. (1994), *Modern Italy: representation and reform*, Routledge, London and New York.

Furnivall, J.S. (1948), *Colonial Policy and Practice: a comparative study of Burma and Netherlands India*, Cambridge, Cambridge.

Gardiner, J.A. and Lyman, T.R. (1978), *Decisions for Sale: corruption and reform in land-use and building regulation*, Praeger, New York.

Garrard, J. (1988-9), 'The Salford gas scandal of 1887', *Manchester Region History Review*, vol. 2, pp. 12-20.

Garrigues, C.H. (1936), *You're paying for it: a guide to graft*, Funk and Wagnall, London and New York.

Geddes, B. and Neto, A.R. (1992), 'International Sources of Corruption in Brazil', *Third World Quarterly*, vol. 13, pp. 601-61.

Gibbon, E. (1776-88), *The History of the Decline and Fall of the Roman Empire*, London.

Gillard, M. and Tomkinson, M. (1980), *Nothing to Declare: the political corruptions of John Poulson*, John Calder, London.

Ginsburgs, G. (1988-89), 'The social and political implications of Soviet crime and corruption', in Shtromas, A. and Kaplan, M. (1988-9), *The Soviet Union and the Challenge of the Future (volume 2)*, Paragon House, New York.

Girling, J.L.S. (1981), *Thailand: society and politics*, Cornell University, Ithaca and London.

Glassner, M.I. (1993), *Political Geography*, Wiley, New York.

Goodman, M. (1974), 'Does political corruption really help economic development?: Yucatan, Mexico', *Polity*, vol. 8, pp. 143-62.

Gorta, A. and Forell, S. (1995), 'Layers of decision: linking social definitions of corruption and willingness to take action', *Crime, Law and Social Change*, vol. 23, pp. 315-43.

Gould, D.J. (1980), *Bureaucratic Corruption and Underdevelopment in the Third World: the case of Zaire*, Pergamon, New York.

Greene, G. (1982), *J'Accuse: the dark side of Nice*, Bodley Head, London.

Greenstone, J.D. (1966), 'Corruption and self interest in Kampala and Nairobi', *Comparative Studies in Society and History*, vol. 8, pp. 199-211.

Grindle, M.S. (1977), *Bureaucrats, Politicians and Peasants in Mexico: a case study in public policy*, University of California, Berkeley.

Hahn, W.G. (1987), *Democracy in a Communist Party: Poland's experience since 1980*, Columbia University, New York.

Hamilton, N. (1982), *The Limits of State Autonomy: post-revolutionary Mexico*, Princeton University, Princeton.

Hann, C.M. (1985), *A Village without Solidarity: Polish peasants in years of crisis*, Yale University, New Haven.

Hansen, R.D. (1971), *The Politics of Mexican Development*, Johns Hopkins, Baltimore.

Hao, Y. and Johnston, M. (1995), 'Reform at the Crossroads: an analysis of Chinese corruption', *Asian Perspective*, vol. 9, pp. 117-50.

Hawksworth, M. and Kogan, M. (1992), *Encyclopaedia of Government and Politics*, Routledge, London and New York.

Heidenheimer, A.J., Johnston, M. and LeVine, V.T. (1989), *Political Corruption: a handbook*, Transaction, New Brunswick. (Referred to in text as Heidenheimer. The most extensive discussion to date. An earlier edition appeared in 1970.)

Heller, A. and Fehér, F. (1988), *The Post-modern Political Condition*, Columbia University, New York.

Hershkowitz, L. (1977), *Tweed's New York: another look*, Anchor, Garden City NY.

Hill, H. (ed) (1994), *Indonesia's New Order: the dynamics of socio-economic transformation*, University of Hawaii, Honolulu.

Holmes, L. (1993), *The End of Communist Power: anti-corruption campaigns and the legitimation crisis*, Polity, Cambridge.

Hook, S. (1980), *Philosophy and Public Policy*, S. Illinois University, Carbondale.

Hope, K.R. (1987), 'Administrative corruption and administrative reform in developing states', *Corruption and Reform*, vol. 2, pp. 127-47.

House of Lords (session 1988-9, paper 27), 5th report, *Standing Committee on the European Community: Fraud against the Community*, House of Lords, London.

Hoyt, E.P. (1991), *The New Japanese: a complacent people in a corrupt society*, Robert Hale, London.

Huberts, L.W.J.C. (1995), 'Public corruption and fraud in the Netherlands: research and results', *Crime, Law and Social Change*, vol. 22, pp. 307-21.

Huntington, S.P. (1968), *Political Order in Changing Societies*, Yale University, New Haven.

Jackson, M. (1988), 'Understanding Police Corruption', *Current Affairs Bulletin*, vol. 65, pp. 30-1.

Jacobs, B. (1984), *Thumbleriggers: the law v. Governor Marvin Mandel*, Johns Hopkins, Baltimore.

Jeejebhoy, Sir J.R.B. (1952), *Bribery and corruption in Bombay*, no publisher given, Bombay.

Jeanneney, J-N. (1982), *L'Argent Caché: milieux d'affaires et pouvoirs politiques dans la France du XXme Siècle*, Fayard, Paris.

Johnston, K.F. (1971), *Mexican Democracy: a critical view*, Allyn and Bacon, Boston.

Johnston, R.J. (1991), *A Question of Place: exploring the practice of human geography*, Blackwell, Oxford.

Jones, E. (1985), 'Politics, bureaucratic corruption and maladministration in the Third World', *International Review of Administrative Sciences*, vol. 51, pp. 19-23.

Judd, D.R. and Mendelson, R.E. (1973), *The Politics of Urban Planning: the East St Louis experience*, Illinois University, Urbana.

Kameir, E.W. and Kursany, I. (1985), 'Corruption as the "fifth" factor of production in the Sudan', *Scandinavian Institute of African Studies*, research report no. 72, Uppsala.

Kaminski, A.Z. (1988), 'The privatization of the state: trends in the evolution of (real) socialist political systems', *Asian Journal of Public Administration*, vol. 10, pp. 27-47.

Kato, S. (ed) (1987), *Government and Politics of Thailand*, Oxford, Oxford.

Katsenelinboigen, A. (1977), 'Coloured markets in the Soviet Union', *Soviet Studies*, vol. 29, pp. 62-85.

Kempe, R.H. (1985), 'Politics, bureaucratic corruption, and maladministration in the Third World', *International Review of Administrative Sciences*, vol. 51, pp. 1-6.

Kennedy, K.H. (1978), *The Mungana Affair*, University of Queensland, St Lucia.

Kjellberg, F. (1995), 'Conflict of interest, corruption or (simply) scandals? The "Oslo case" 1989-91', *Crime, Law and Social Change*, vol. 22, pp. 539-60.

Klitgaard, R. (1984), 'Managing the case against corruption: a case study', *Public Administration and Development*, vol. 4, pp. 77-98.

Klitgaard, R. (1988), *Controlling Corruption*, California University, Berkeley.

Kochanowicz, J. (1993), 'Transition to market in a comparative perspective', in Poznanski, K.Z. (ed) (1993), *Stabilization and Privatisation in Poland*, Kluwer, Boston. (*International Studies in Economics and Econometrics*, vol. 29.)

Kramer, J.M. (1977), 'Political Corruption in the USSR', *Western Political Quarterly*, vol. 30, pp. 213-24.

Kummer, D.M. (1995), 'The political use of Philippine forestry statistics in the postwar period', *Crime, Law and Social Change*, vol. 22, pp. 163-80.

Lamine, S. (1979), *Princes Africaines*, Hallier, Paris.

Langan, P. and Cooksey, B. (1995), *The National Integrity System in Tanzania*, Economic Development Institute of the World Bank, no place of publication given. (The proceedings of a Transparency International workshop.)

La Polambara, J. (1964), *Interest Groups in Italian Politics*, Princeton University, Princeton.

Latin American Regional Reports Mexico and NAFTA (1993-), Latin American Newsletters, London. (Published as *Latin America Regional Reports Mexico and Central America 1979-92*. Equivalent series exist for the remainder of the Americas.)

Leff, N.H. (1964), 'Economic development through bureaucratic corruption', *American Behavioral Scientist*, vol. 8, pp. 8-14.

Lesnik, R. and Blanc, H. (1990), *L'Empire Corrompu*, Robert Laffont, Paris.

Lethbridge, H.J. (1985), *Hard graft in Hong Kong: scandal, corruption, the ICAC*, Oxford, Oxford.

LeVine, V.T. (1975), *Political Corruption: the Ghana case*, Hoover Institution, Stanford.

Lissak, M. (1976), *Military Roles in Modernisation: civil-military relations in Thailand and Burma*, Sage, Beverly Hills and London.

Little, W. (1992), 'Political corruption in Latin America', *Corruption and Reform*, vol. 7, pp. 41-66.

Lui, F.T. (1996), 'Three aspects of corruption', *Contemporary Economic Policy*, vol. 14, pp. 26-9.

MacDougall, T. (1988), 'The Lockheed scandal and the high cost of politics in Japan', in Markovits, A.S. and Silverstein, M. (1988), *The Politics of Scandal: power and process in liberal democracies*, Holmes and Meier, New York, pp. 193-229.

MacGaffey, J. (1987), *Entrepreneurs and Parasites: the struggle for indigenous capitalism in Zaire*, Cambridge, Cambridge.

McKinnon, J. (1992), 'Can the Military be sidelined? (Thailand)', *Pacific Viewpoint*, vol. 33, pp. 128-34.

McKitrick, E.L. (1987), 'The Study of Corruption', *Political Science Quarterly*, vol. 72, pp. 502-14.

McMullen, M. (1961), 'A theory of corruption', *Sociological Review*, vol. 9 (new series), pp. 181-201.

Madsen, A. (1990), *Silk Roads: the Asian adventures of Clara and André Malraux*, Tauris, London.

Maiden, A.N. (1991), 'Construction's Big Hole in Your Pocket', *Independent Monthly* (Surry Hills N.S.W.), vol. 2, pp. 261-2.

Malec, K.L. and Gardiner, J.A. (1987), 'Measurement issues in the study of official corruption: a Chicago example', *Corruption and Reform*, vol. 2, pp. 267-78.

Mandelbaum, S.J. (1965), *Boss Tweed's New York*, Wiley, New York.

Markovits, A.S. and Silverstein, M. (eds) (1988), *The Politics of Scandal*, Holmes and Meier, New York and London.

Mason, D.S. (1985), *Public Opinion and Political Change in Poland, 1980-82*, Cambridge, Cambridge.

Massock, R.G. (1943), *Italy from Within*, Macmillan, London.

Mauro, P. (1995), 'Corruption and growth', *Quarterly Journal of Economics*, vol. 110, pp. 681-712.

Mèdard, J.F. (1986), 'Public corruption in Africa: a comparative perspective', *Corruption and Reform*, vol. 1, pp. 115-31.

Mèdard, J.F. (1990), review of Bayart, J-F. (1989), *L'etat en Afrique: la politique du ventre*, Fayart, Paris, in *Corruption and Reform*, vol. 5, pp. 71-5.

Merton, R.K. (1949), *Social Theory and Social Structure*, Free Press, Glencoe, Illinois.

Mitchell, D. (1970), 'Wanokalada: a case study in local administration', *Bulletin of Indonesian Economic Studies*, vol. 6, pp. 76-93.

Momsen, W.J. (1974), *The Age of Bureaucracy: perspectives on the political sociology of Max Weber*, Blackwell, Oxford.

Monteiro, J.B. (1966), *Corruption: control of maladministration*, Manaktalas, Bombay.

Morell, D. and Samudavanijah, C. (1981), *Political Conflict in Thailand: reform, reaction and revolution*, Oelgeschlager Gunn and Hain, Cambridge.

Morton, H. (1980), 'Who gets what, when and how? Housing in the Soviet Union', *Soviet Studies*, vol. 32, pp. 235-59.

Mosley, C. (1984), Review of Doig, A. (1984), *Corruption and Misconduct in Contemporary British Politics*, Penguin, London, in *Political Quarterly*, vol. 55, pp. 339-41.

Murata, K. (1979), *Japan: the state of the nation*, Japan Times, Tokyo.

Mya Maung (1990), 'The Burma Road from the Union of Burma to Myanmar', *Asian Survey*, vol. 30, pp. 602-24.

Mya Maung (1991), *The Burma Road to Poverty*, Praeger, New York.

Myrdal, G. (1968), *Asian Drama: an inquiry into the poverty of nations*, Penguin, London.

Nadelmann, E.A. (1987-8), 'The DEA in Latin America: dealing with institutionalised corruption', *Journal of Inter-American Studies and World Affairs*, vol. 29, pp. 1-39.

Neher, C.D. (1977), 'Political corruption in a Thai province', *Journal of Developing Areas*, vol. 11, pp. 479-92.

New York Times (1858-), New York.

Noonan, J.T. (1984), *Bribes*, Macmillan, New York.

Neue Zürcher Zeitung (1780-), Zurich.

O'Brien, P. (ed) (1986), *The Burke Ambush: corporatism and civil society in West Australia*, Apollo, Perth.

O'Brien, P. (1988), 'West Australia Inc.: a state of corruption', *Quadrant*, vol. 32, pp. 4-18.

O'Brien, P. (1990), 'The last laugh: Western Australia's elections and the executive state, 1983-89', *Politics*, vol. 25, pp. 113-30.

Observer, The (1791-), London.

Ockey, J. (1994), 'Political parties, factions and corruption in Thailand', *Modern Asian Studies*, vol. 28, pp. 251-78.

O'Connor, A. (1991), *Poverty in Africa: a geographical approach*, Belhaven, London.

Olowu, D. (1985), 'Bureaucratic corruption and public accountability in Nigeria: an assessment of recent developments', *International Review of Administrative Sciences*, vol. 51, pp. 7-12.

Panda, B. (1978), *Indian Bureaucracy: an inside story*, Uppal, New Delhi.

Panter-Brick, K. (ed) (1978), *Soldiers and Oil: the political transformation of Nigeria*, Frank Cass (*Studies in Commonwealth Politics and History*, no. 5), London.

Parker, R.S. (1978), *The government of New South Wales*, Queensland University, St Lucia.

Passas, N. and Nelken, D. (1993), 'The thin line between legitimate and criminal enterprises: subsidy frauds in the European Community, *Crime, Law and Social Change*, vol. 19, pp. 223-44.

Perry, P.J. (1990), 'Les Samoa: esquisse d'une géographie politique', *Cahiers d'Outre-Mer*, vol. 43, pp. 189-204.

Perry, P.J. (1993), 'Military Rule in Burma: a geographical analysis', *Crime, Law and Social Change*, vol. 19, pp. 17-32.

Perry, P.J. (1994), 'Corruption and Geography: a fable', *Applied Geography*, vol. 14, pp. 291-3.

Pinto-Duschinsky, M. (1977), 'Corruption in Britain: the Royal Commission on Standards of Conduct in Public Life', *Political Studies*, vol. 25, pp. 274-84.

Pounds, N.J.G. (1972), *Political Geography* (2nd edition), McGraw-Hill, New York.

Prasser, S., Wear, R. and Nethercole, J. (1990), *Corruption and reform: the Fitzgerald vision*, Queensland University, St Lucia.

The Press (1861-), Christchurch, New Zealand.

Price, R. (1975), *Society and Bureaucracy in Contemporary Ghana*, University of California, Berkeley.

Quah, J.S.T. (1988), 'Corruption in Asia with special reference to Singapore: patterns and consequences', *Asian Journal of Public Administration*, vol. 10, pp. 80-95.

Quah, J.S.T. (1995), 'Controlling corruption in city-states: a comparative study of Hong Kong and Singapore', *Crime, Law and Social Change*, vol. 22, pp. 391-414.

Ray, J.K. (1972), *Portraits of Thai politics*, Longman, New Delhi.

Reed, Q. (1995), 'Transition, dysfunctionality and change in the Czech and Slovak republics', *Crime, Law and Social Change*, vol. 22, pp. 323-37.

Report of the Special Committee for eradication of corruption from services (1981), Islamabad. (A misprint for 1961.)

Reisman, W.M. (1979), *Folded Lies: bribery, crusades and reform*, Free Press, New York.

Revel, J-F. (1987), 'Paris notebook - the varieties of corruption', *Encounter*, vol. 68, pp. 36-8.

Rogow, A.A. and Lasswell, H.D. (1963), *Power, Corruption and Rectitude*, Prentice Hall, Englewood Cliffs NJ.

Ronfeldt, D. (1973), *Atencuigo: the politics of agrarian struggle in a Mexican ejido*, Stanford University, Stanford.

Rose-Ackerman, S. (1978), *Corruption: a study in political economy*, Academic, New York.

Rostovtzeff, M. (1957), *The Social and Economic History of the Roman Empire* (2 vols), Clarendon, Oxford.

Royal Commission on the Activities of the Federal Ship Painters and Dockers Union (1984) (6 vols), Government Printer, Canberra.

Russell, B. (Lord) (1938), *Power: a new social analysis*, Allen and Unwin, London.

Sandbrook, R. with Barker, J. (1985), *The Politics of Africa's Economic Stagnation*, Cambridge, Cambridge.

Sandercock, L. (1979), *The Land Racket: the real costs of property speculation*, Hale and Iremonger, Sydney.

Santharam Committee (1970), Report of the Committee on Prevention of Corruption (India), New Delhi.

Sarassoro, H. (1980), *La Corruption des Fonctionaires en Afrique: étude de droit pénal comparé*, Economica, Paris.

Sauer, C.O. (1941), 'Foreword to historical geography', *Annals of the Association of American Geographers*, vol. 31, p. 4.

Schleifer, A. and Vishny, R.W. (1993), 'Corruption', *Quarterly Journal of Economics*, vol. 108, pp. 599-617.

Scott, J.C. (1972), *Comparative Political Corruption*, Prentice Hall, Englewood Cliffs NJ.

Scott, T., Carstairs, A. and Roots, D. (1988), 'Corruption prevention: the Hong Kong approach', *Asian Journal of Public Administration*, vol. 10, pp. 110-19.

Shalid Alam, M. (1989), 'Anatomy of Corruption: an approach to the political economy of underdevelopment', *American Journal of Economics and Sociology*, vol. 48, pp. 441-56.

Shapley, R.E. (1889-new edition), *Solid for Mulhooly: a political satire*, Gebbie, Philadelphia.

Shtromas, A. and Kaplan, M.A. (1988-9), *The Soviet Union and the Challenge of the Future* (4 vols), Paragon, New York.

Shwe Lu Maung (1989), *Burma: nationalism and ideology - an analysis of society, culture and politics*, Dhaka University, Dhaka.

Siemenska, R. and Tarkowski, J. (1980), 'Polish local leaders and fulfilling community needs: politicians or administrators?', *International Political Science Review*, vol. 1, pp. 244-64.

Simis, K.M. (1982), *USSR: secrets of a corrupt society*, Dent, London.

Skolnick, J.H. (1992), 'Rethinking the drug problem', *Daedalus*, vol. 121, pp. 133-59.

Slowe, P.M. (1990), *Geography and Political Power: the geography of nations and states*, Routledge, London and New York.

Smith, M.G. (1964), 'Historical and cultural conditions of political corruption among the Hausa', *Comparative Studies in Society and History*, vol. 6, pp. 164-94.

South East Asia Monitor (1990-), London.

Stead, W.T. (1894), *If Christ came to Chicago*, Review of Reviews, London.

Steffens, J.L. (1904), *The Shame of the Cities*, McClure Phillips, New York.

Steinberg, D.I. (1981), *Burma's road toward development: growth and ideology under military rule*, Westview, Boulder.

Steinberg, D.I. (1990), 'International rivalries in Burma: the rise of economic competition', *Asian Survey*, vol. 30, pp. 587-601.

Steinberg, D.I. (1991), 'Democracy, power and the economy in Burma: donor dilemmas', *Asian Survey*, vol. 31, pp. 729-42.

Steinberg, D.I. (1992), 'Myanmar in 1991: the miasma in Burma', *Asian Survey*, vol. 32, pp. 146-53.

Steketee, M. and Cockburn, M. (1980), *Wran: an unauthorised biography*, Allen & Unwin, Sydney.

Stockwin, J.A.A. (1975), *Japan: divided politics in a growth economy*, Weidenfeld and Nicholson, London.

Story, D. (1986), *The Mexican ruling party: stability and authority*, Praeger, New York.

Streek, B. and Wicksteed, R. (1981), *Render unto Kaiser*, Ravan, Johannesburg.

Sucharithanarugse, W. (1984), 'The idea of power in Thai society', in Tearweil, B.J. (ed) (1984), *Development issues in Thailand* (First international conference on Thai studies, 1981, New Delhi), Centre for South-East Asian Studies, Gaya.

Summers, M.W. (1987), *The Plundering Generation: corruption and the crisis of the Union*, Oxford, Oxford.

Taras, R. (1986), *Poland: socialist state, rebellious nation*, Westview, Boulder.

Tarkowski, J. (1981), 'Poland: patrons and clients in a planned economy', in Eisenstadt, S.N. and Lemarchand, R. (1981), *Political clientelism, patronage and development*, Sage, Beverly Hills.

Tarkowski, J. (1983), 'Patronage in a centralised socialist system: the case of Poland', *International Political Science Review*, vol. 4, pp. 495-518.

Tarkowski, J. (1988), 'A centralised system and corruption: the case of Poland', *Journal of Public Administration*, vol. 10, pp. 48-68.

Taylor, P.J. (1987), *The State in Burma*, University of Hawaii, Honolulu.

Taylor, P.J. (1993), *Political Geography: world-economy, nation-state and locality* (3rd edition), Longman, Harlow.

Temby, I. (1990), 'Tailing corruption in New South Wales', *University of New South Wales Law Journal*, vol. 13, pp. 137-46.

Than, M. and Tan, J.L.H. (1990), *Myanmar dilemmas and options: the challenge of economic transition in the 1990s*, ASEAN/Institute of Southeast Asian Studies, Singapore.

Theobald, R. (1990), *Corruption, Development and Underdevelopment*, Macmillan, London.

Ting Gong (1994), *The Politics of Corruption in Contemporary China*, Praeger, Westport.

Transparency International (1994), *Accountability and Transparency in International Economic Development*, German Foundation for International Development and Transparency International, Berlin.

Ugalde, A. (1970), *Power and Conflict in a Mexican city*, University of New Mexico, Albuquerque.

van der Meer, C.L.H. (1981), *Rural development in northern Thailand*, Kuips, Groningen.

van Wolferen, K. (1990), *The Enigma of Power: people and politics in a stateless nation*, Knopf, New York.

Veyne, P. (1981), 'Clientèle et corruption au service de l'Etat: la vénalité des offices dans le Bas Empire romain', *Annales: économie-societé-civilization*, vol. 36, pp. 339-61.

Wade, R. (1982), 'The system of administrative and political corruption: canal irrigation in south India', *Journal of Development Studies*, vol. 18, pp. 289-328.

Wade, R. (1984), 'The market for public office: why the Indian state is not better at development', Institute of Development Studies, University of Sussex, Brighton, discussion paper 194, July 1984.

Walton, J. and Seddon, D. (1994), *Free markets and food riots: the politics of global adjustment*, Blackwell, Oxford.

Waquet, J-C. (1991), *Corruption: ethics and power in Florence: 1600-1770*, Polity, Cambridge.

Ward, P. (1986), *Welfare politics in Mexico: papering over the cracks*, Allen and Unwin, London.

Ward, P.M. (ed) (1989), *Corruption, development and inequality: soft touch or hard graft*, Routledge, London.

Warren, R.P. (1946), *All the King's Men*, Harcourt, New York.

Waterbury, J. (1973), 'Endemic and Planned Corruption in a Monarchical Regime', *World Politics*, vol. 25, pp. 533-55.

Wedel, J. (1986), *The Private Poland*, Facts on File, New York.

Whetten, N.L. (1948), *Rural Mexico*, University of Chicago, Chicago.

Whip, R. and Hughes, C.A. (eds) (1991), *Political Crossroads: the 1989 Queensland election*, Queensland University, St Lucia.

White, S. (1995), 'A variable geometry of enforcement? Aspects of European Community budget fraud', *Crime, Law and Social Change*, vol. 23, pp. 235-55.

Williams, R. (1986), 'Crime and corruption in Australia', *Corruption and Reform*, vol. 1, pp. 101-13.

Williams, R. (1987), *Political corruption in Africa*, Gower, Aldershot.

Wilson, J.Q. (1966), 'Corruption: the shame of the states', *The Public Interest*, vol. 2, pp. 28-38.

Wing Lo, T. (1993), *Corruption and Politics in Hong Kong and China*, Open University, Buckingham and Philadelphia.

Wraith, R.E. and Simpkins, E. (1963), *Corruption in developing countries*, Allen and Unwin, London.

Wrong, D. (ed) (1970), *Max Weber*, Prentice Hall, Englewood Cliffs.

Wyatt, D.K. (1984), *Thailand: a short history*, Yale University, New Haven.

Xie Baoqui (1988), 'The function of the Chinese procuratorial organ in the combat against corruption', *Australian Journal of Public Administration*, vol. 10, pp. 71-9.

Index

References from Notes indicated by 'n' after page preference